OUTDOOR ED
TEACHING ST

Increase Student Engagement
While Transforming Your Teaching

Christian Bisson
Julie Gabert Bisson

Illustrations by Meg McAndrew

Outdoor Education Teaching Strategies

Outdoor Education Teaching Strategies
© 2020 Christian Bisson and Julie Gabert Bisson

ISBN: 9781653290000
Library of Congress Control Number: 2020900008
All rights reserved. No part of this publication may be reproduced or transmitted in any form or by any mechanical means including information storage and retrieval systems without written permission from the authors, except by a reviewer who may quote brief passages in a review.

Illustrated by Meg McAndrew

Nuannaarpoq Publishing
Plymouth, NH, USA

Dedicated

*To all of our past, present and future
students and co-instructors.
Thank you for inspiring us to be better teachers.*

And

*To Luc and Lia,
our greatest teachers!*

Nuannaarpoq!

*"Taking extravagant pleasure
in being alive!"*

*An Inuit word that has shaped our philosophy of life &
learning for over 30 years. May this book inspire you to take
extravagant pleasure in living, learning, and teaching!*

Content

INTRODUCTION 8

LEARNING & TEACHING THEORIES 10
- LEARNING THEORIES 11
- LEARNING MODELS 22
- THE PEDAGOGY OF FUN 42

PLANNING YOUR TEACHING 46
- CREATING A SAFE LEARNING ENVIRONMENT 47
- OUTDOOR TEACHING CONSIDERATIONS 51
- MANAGING GROUPS OUTDOORS 56
- THREE TYPES OF LESSONS TAUGHT OUTDOORS 65
- BEING A REFLECTIVE TEACHER 68
- USING PROPS AND VISUAL AIDS TO ENHANCE LEARNING 70
- TEACHING MECHANICS 73
- GETTING STARTED: PLANNING AND PREPARATION 79

TEACHING OUTDOOR EXPEDITION-BASED EXPERIENCES 82
- THE GRASSHOPPER APPROACH TO CURRICULUM PLANNING 83
- PLANNING THE FIRST 72 HOURS 86
- LENGTH OF A LESSON 88
- USING TEACHABLE MOMENTS 89

TEACHING STRATEGIES 91
- TEACHING STYLES VS. TEACHING STRATEGIES 92
- SKILL ORIENTED TEACHING STRATEGIES 94

  - *EDP - ECP* *95*
  - *Step by Step* *102*
  - *Whole - Part - Whole* *106*
  - *Physical Manipulation* *108*
  - *Prompting Cues* *110*
  - *Video Feedback* *112*

- KNOWLEDGE ORIENTED TEACHING STRATEGIES 114

  - *Interactive Lecture* *115*
  - *Lecture with Seeded Questions* *119*
  - *Lecture with Seeded Facts* *122*
  - *Lecture with Seeded Q-cards* *124*

Leapfrogging *126*
Mystery Challenge *129*
Demonstration *132*
Skill Modeling *134*
Scale Modeling *135*
Guided Discovery *139*

VALUE ORIENTED TEACHING STRATEGIES 143

Quotes and Readings *144*
Personal Journaling *146*
Group Journaling *148*
Visual (Guided) Imagery *151*
Case Study *153*
Nature Awareness Activities *156*

MULTI ORIENTED TEACHING STRATEGIES 158

Art *159*
Music *161*
Storytelling *163*
Student Storytelling *166*
Puppetry *168*
Student Puppetry *171*
Role-Play *173*
Theatrics *175*
Skits *178*
Role Modeling *181*
Discussion *182*
Debate *184*
Exploratory Learning *186*
Socratic Method *188*
Games *189*
Problem Solving Activities *192*
Simulation *195*
Solo Experience *196*
Peer Teaching *198*
Service Learning *199*

ASSESSMENT 201

WHY ASSESS STUDENTS 202
ASSESSING STUDENT LEARNING 203
ASSESSING STUDENT SKILLS 206

Assessing Student Content Knowledge	211
Assessing Student Values	216

APPENDIX 218

Lesson Plan Preface	219
Sample Lesson Plan for Teaching a Technical Skill	220
Sample Lesson Plan for Teaching Content Knowledge	226
Sample Lesson Plan for Teaching Values	234
Outdoor Teaching Strategy Field Summary	238

REFERENCES 242
ABOUT THE AUTHORS 245

Introduction

After more than 65 years of combined teaching in the outdoors and teaching how to teach outdoors, we have learned a few tricks on how to engage learners and help them acquire new skills, knowledge, and values.

During these years of working in Outdoor Education we have seen the outdoor profession produce plenty of research along with articles and books on outdoor skill development, leadership, and risk management. However, little has been written on how to teach.

It is common for young outdoor educators to imitate the type of teaching that they have been exposed to. If they have seen teachers lecture in or outside the classroom, they often use the same lecturing strategy to deliver their own lessons. This behavior is normal. Effective and engaging teaching is predominantly a learned skill that often needs to be acquired through training, experience, feedback and reflection.

The reality of teacher training is simple. We know that exposing young outdoor educators to engaging, creative and effective teaching often inspires them to enact good teaching. Conversely, exposing young educators to mediocre, boring and ineffective teaching often leads to teachers delivering dull, forgettable lessons.

The purpose of this book is to share our passion for excellence in teaching while helping others improve their own teaching. We seek to explain the art and science of teaching outdoors while giving future and seasoned educators concrete teaching strategies and tips to improve one's own teaching. Whether you teach month long wilderness education expeditions, week long residential outdoor education courses, intensive weekend adventure education classes, environmental education day programs, or year-round school curriculums that integrate outdoor learning, this book will allow you to expand and improve your teaching repertoire. And although this book was written for educators using outdoor classrooms, the teaching strategies presented in this text could also be effectively transferred to indoor classrooms.

The book is divided into five sections. The first provides a foundation for understanding relevant theories and research explaining how students learn best and what teachers can do to be effective outdoor educators. The second is dedicated to planning effective and engaging lessons. The third addresses considerations for an expedition-based curriculum. The fourth section makes up the bulk of the book by presenting 42 distinct teaching strategies suitable for instructing skills, knowledge, or value related lessons. The fifth and final section presents various ways to assess student learning. We have also included an appendix with sample lesson plans and a printable quick reference sheet to take into the field.

We included many field-tested practical teaching tips and strategies that we use regularly in our own outdoor teaching. Some are classics, some we picked up years ago from many wonderful co-instructors along our teaching journey, some we improved through our trials and errors, and others we created over time.

We organized these strategies into three broad lesson topic categories to help you select the appropriate teaching strategy based on your goals. The categories are **skills**, **knowledge**, and **values**. You will see us reference these categories throughout the book.

We included our organizational structure called the **Teaching Strategy Level of Active Engagement Model** which was inspired by the American educator Edgar Dale. In our adaptation of Dale's Cone of Experience, we assign a value based on the learner's level of engagement during each teaching strategy ranging from passive to active. The model is designed to help you choose a teaching strategy based on your lesson topic, time, situation, and the level of experience (passive to active) that you choose to engage your students.

In the end, we hope that this text will allow you to discover new teaching strategies, reacquaint yourself with old teaching tricks, and inspire you to invent new ways of teaching effectively in the outdoors. It is our vision that with more experience and reflection on your own teaching, you will be inspired to use or adapt these strategies to your own lessons to become the best possible teacher you can be.

CHAPTER 1

Learning & Teaching Theories

Learning Theories

Learning Models

The Pedagogy of Fun

Learning Theories

Teaching in the outdoors is a wonderful combination of science and art. The science supporting outdoor education is the same as the science supporting good effective education. Good teaching can occur in a classroom or outside the classroom. Therefore, you will see in this chapter some classic learning and teaching theories that have not emerged from outdoor, environmental, or adventure education academic research. Yet, these theories are pertinent to you as an outdoor educator since the teaching strategies showcased in this book are often good strategies for implementing elements of these theories.

For this text, we have selected some of the most pertinent, well established, or most cutting-edge learning and teaching theories. Our selection includes:

- Constructivist Learning Theory
- Brain-based Learning Theory
- Multiple Intelligences Theory
- Growth Mindset Theory
- Maslow's Hierarchy of Needs Theory

Remember, understanding how your students learn is essential to achieving your goal to be an effective educator. These theories should inform and influence your practice.

Constructivist Learning Theory

Constructivist Learning Theory (CLT) is one of the most accepted, prevalent and influential learning theories in educational settings. It influences many public, private, formal and informal learning programs, elementary schools, high schools, colleges and universities.

CLT is often perceived as a philosophy and not just a theoretical construct explaining how students learn. Because of this, it has been adopted by progressive educators since the early 1900's with the work of John Dewey (1859–1952), the rediscovered writing of Lev Vygotsky (1896–1934), and most importantly the research of Jean Piaget (1896–1980) on children's play and developmental phases.

In a nutshell, CTL propose that the learner constructs new knowledge, skills or values through experiences which are integrated via two processes, (1) *assimilation* and (2) *accommodation*. It also infers that the leaner is not an "empty vessel" who needs to be filled with new knowledge. On the contrary, teachers who embrace CLT understand that their students have life experiences which inform their perception of the world. From this perspective, CLT implies that the role of the teacher is to help guide the learner to discover or acquire new knowledge constructed upon their existing knowledge bank. Again, this construction of new knowledge, skills or values is performed via the process of *assimilation* or *accommodation*.

When students assimilate new information, they incorporate it into an already existing framework without changing the framework. On the other hand, when students learn through accommodation, they change that framework to fit new knowledge presented via experiences. Contrarily to the assimilation process, accommodation allows student to learn from the experience of failure.

Educational concepts characteristic of CLT can also be found in educational approaches such as Place-based Education and Waldorf Schools (Rudolf Steiner, 1861-1925).

From a practical point of view, CLT informs us that as teachers we can use teaching strategies that engage the learners via challenges or proper questioning. As you will see in Chapter 4, teaching strategies such as *Guided Discovery*, *Problem Solving Activities*, *Mystery Challenge*, *Lecture with Seeded Q-Cards*, and *Discussion* are only a few examples of teaching strategies that embrace the idea that your students are not "empty vessels" but in reality they are full of information, facts, experiences, and ideas that can help them construct new knowledge, skills, or values.

Brain-based Learning Theory

Brain-based Learning Theory (BBLT), also known as Natural Learning Theory, refers to an educational approach which is based on the latest scientific research about how the brain learns.

A great deal of the scientific research and academic dialogue related to brain-based learning has been focused on neuroplasticity—the concept that neural connections in the brain change, remap, and reorganize themselves when people learn new concepts, have new experiences, or practice certain skills over time. Scientists have also determined that the brain can perform several activities at once; that the same information can be stored in multiple areas of the brain; that learning functions can be affected by diet, exercise, stress, and other conditions; that meaning is more important than information when the brain is learning something new; and that certain emotional states can facilitate or impede learning—among many other findings.

According to two leading education scholars, Renate Caine and Geoffrey Caine, Brain-based "Natural" Learning research findings inform us that instructional strategies should aim to create the following learning environment:

1. **Orchestrated Immersion in Complex Experiences** - Creating learning environments that fully immerse students in educational and complex experiences.
2. **Relaxed Alertness** -Trying to eliminate fear in learners, while maintaining a highly challenging environment.
3. **Active Processing** -Allowing the learner to consolidate and internalize information by actively processing it.

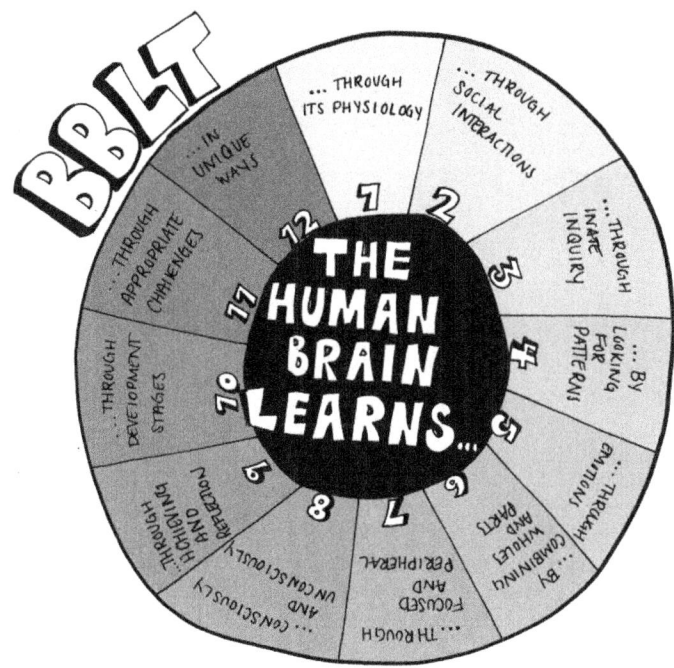

Caine & Caine's Brain-based / Natural Learning Theory

Consequently, you should immerse your students in complex, interactive experiences that are both rich and real, which an outdoor classroom can easily provide. To enhance motivation in learning, try presenting your students with personally meaningful challenges and selecting lesson topics that are relevant to your students. In order for your students to gain insight about a problem or a situation, provide them with opportunities to "actively processes" the different ways to solve a problem or analyze a situation.

Caine and Caine also came up with 12 principles based on BBLT research. You can find these 12 principles in the figure above. To further your understanding of these 12 principles, we invite you to read the work of Caine and Caine.

In our practice as educators, BBLT informs us that we can use teaching strategies that engage learners via meaningful challenges with an openness to failure. As you will see in chapter 4, teaching strategies such as *Problem Solving Activities*, *Simulations*, *Video Feedback*, *Case Studies*, *Exploratory Learning*, *Solo Experiences*, *Peer Teaching*, and *Service Learning* are good examples of teaching strategies that support the principles of Brain-based Learning Theory.

Multiple Intelligence Theory

In 1983 Howard Gardner wrote a book titled: *Frames of Mind: The Theory of Multiple Intelligences*. Since then, the education profession has largely accepted his theoretical model of multiple intelligences. Gardner's research shows that along with the biology of the brain, culture also plays a significant role in the development of particular intelligences. Gardner currently has identified nine distinct intelligences all of which are needed for humans to function in society. By teaching to or providing learning experiences in these intelligences, deeper meaning and understanding can often be achieved.

Gardner's Multiple Intelligence Theory

Gardner's Multiple Intelligence Learner Characteristics

Bodily-Kinesthetic (Body)
- Likes to move around, touch and talk, uses body language and facial expression.
- Is good at physical activities and crafts.
- Learns best by touching, moving, interacting with space, and processing knowledge through bodily sensations.

Interpersonal (People)
- Likes to have lots of friends, talk to people, join groups, and work collaboratively.
- Is good at understanding people, leading others, organizing, communicating, manipulating and mediating conflicts.
- Learns best by sharing, comparing, relating, cooperating and interviewing

Intrapersonal (Self)
- Likes to work alone and pursue own interests.
- Is good at understanding self, focusing inward on feelings and dreams, following instincts, being original.
- Learns best by working alone, individualized projects, self-paced instruction, and personal space.

Logical-Mathematical (Logic)
- Likes to do experiments, work with numbers, and explore patterns and relationships between variables.
- Is good at math, reasoning, logic and problem solving.
- Learns best by categorizing, classifying and working with abstract patterns or relationships.

Verbal-Linguistic (Word)
- Likes to read, write and tell stories.
- Is good at memorizing names, places, dates and trivia.
- Learns best by saying, hearing and seeing words.

Visual-Spatial (Art)
- Likes to draw, build, design and create things; look at pictures, slides, movies; play with machines.
- Is good at imagining things, sensing changes, working with mazes or puzzles, reading maps and charts.
- Learns best by visualizing, imagining, working with colors and images.

Musical-Rhythmic and Harmonic (Music)
- Likes to sing or hum tunes; listen to music, play an instrument, move with music.
- Is good at picking up sounds, remembering melodies, noticing pitches and rhythms, keeping time.
- Learns best by rhythm, melody and music.

Naturalistic (Nature)
- Likes to be outside, with animals, geography and weather, interacting with surroundings.
- Is good at noticing patterns and characteristics in environment, distinguishing animals and plants from each other, sensing natural changes.
- Learns best by studying natural phenomenon, working in a natural setting, learning how things work, categorizing things.

Existential (Meta)
- Likes to experience meaningful learning, look for connections across the curriculum, enjoy literature and customs from other cultures, express a sense of belonging to a global community, and like to get involved with social and political causes.
- Is good at seeing the big picture, building and supporting community.
- Learns best by processing the experience, reflecting through journaling and blogging.

Gardner's nine intelligences are listed in the tables below. The left columns identify various teaching strategies that cater to each intelligence. This is varies greatly depending on how the class is run.

Gardner's theory of multiple intelligences acknowledges the varied learning abilities and talents of students. It is possible to engage multiple intelligences in one single lesson by including a variety of teaching strategies. By doing so, you can promote deeper engagement and learning for more students.

Teaching Strategies and Gardner's Nine Intelligences

Garner's Intelligences	1	2	3	4	5	6	7	8	9
Skill Oriented Strategies									
EDP - ECP	X			X	X				
Step by Step	X			X	X				
Whole-Part-Whole	X			X	X				
Physical Manipulation	X			X	X				
Prompting Cues	X			X	X				
Video Feedback	X			X	X				
Knowledge Oriented Strategies									
Interactive Lecture		X		X	X				
Lecture Seeded Question		X		X	X				
Lecture Seeded Facts		X		X	X				
Lecture Seeded Q-Cards		X		X	X				
Leapfrogging		X		X	X			X	
Mystery Challenge		X		X	X			X	
Demonstration				X	X				
Skill Modeling	X	X		X					
Scale Modeling	X	X		X	X			X	X
Guided Discovery		X		X	X			X	
Value Oriented Strategies									
Quotes and Readings		X	X		X			X	X
Personal Journaling			X		X	X		X	X
Group Journaling		X	X		X	X		X	X
Visual (Guided) Imagery			X		X			X	X
Case Study		X		X	X				
Nature Awareness	X		X			X		X	X

Gardner's Multiple Intelligences
Body (1), People (2), Self (3), Logic (4), Word (5), Art (6), Music (7), Nature (8), Meta (9)

Teaching Strategies and Gardner's Nine Intelligences

Garner's Intelligences	1	2	3	4	5	6	7	8	9
Multi Oriented Strategies									
Art	X	X	X			X		X	X
Music	X	X	X	X	X	X	X	X	X
Storytelling						X		X		X
Student Storytelling	X	X	X			X	X	X		X
Puppetry						X	X	X		
Student Puppetry	X	X	X			X	X	X		
Role-Play	X	X				X	X	X		
Theatrics	X	X				X	X	X		
Skits	X	X				X	X	X		
Role Modeling		X								
Discussion		X			X					X
Debate		X		X	X					X
Exploratory Learning	X	X	X						X	X
Socratic Method			X	X	X					X
Games	X	X		X	X					
Problem Solving Activities	X	X	X	X	X					
Simulations	X	X		X	X					
Solo Experience	X		X						X	X
Peer Teaching	X	X			X					
Service Learning	X	X	X							X

Gardner's Multiple Intelligences
Body (1), People (2), Self (3), Logic (4), Word (5), Art (6), Music (7), Nature (8), Meta (9)

Growth Mindset Theory

The concept of a growth mindset was developed by American psychologist Carol Dweck and popularized in her book, *Mindset: The New Psychology of Success* published in 2007. In recent years, many schools and educators have started using Dweck's theories to inform how they teach students.

According to Dweck, a mindset can be identified as "a fixed mindset" or "a growth mindset." A simple definition of the concept proposed by Dweck reads, "A mindset is a self-perception that people hold about themselves."

Believing that you are either "good at rock climbing" or "bad at rock climbing" is an example of a fixed-mindset, while believing that one can improve one's climbing skills by putting time and effort into climbing harder routes is an example of a growth mindset. According to Dweck, students can be aware or unaware of their mindsets. What is important to remember is that either way, one's mindset will have a profound effect on one's learning achievement, skill acquisition, personal relationships, professional success, and many other dimensions of life.

Dweck's research suggests that students who have adopted a fixed mindset—for instance the belief that they are either "competent" or "incompetent" and that there is no way to change this—may be inclined not to try to learn new skills or may learn skills at a much slower rate. These students also tend to shy away from challenges. Dweck's findings also suggest that when students with fixed mindsets fail at something, as everyone eventually does, they will be more inclined to tell themselves they can't or won't be able to learn a new skill. They might say to others or themselves "I just can't learn how to tie knots" or "I can't learn the name of all these flowers" or "I can't learn how to use a compass."

Alternatively, "In a growth mindset, people believe that their most basic abilities can be developed through dedication and hard work—brains and talent are just the starting point. This view creates a love of learning and a resilience that is essential for great accomplishment," writes Dweck. Students who are exposed to appropriate challenges in a supportive environment will most likely embrace a growth mindset.

As seen above in the section on brain-based learning theory, research on how the brain learns supports the concept of "relax alertness" which is proven to be essential for favoring learning and growth. The Growth Mindset Theory reinforces this concept and should always be on your mind as you create lessons in outdoor education. Ideally, these merging theories should inform your lesson planning as well as the learning environment that you create on every course or expedition you lead.

The take home message from Dweck's work on Growth Mindset is that the delineation between fixed and growth mindsets has potentially far-reaching implications for classroom and outdoor teachers, since the ways in which students think about learning and their own abilities can have a significant effect on their own learning progress and academic improvement. If you encourage your students to believe that they can learn more and become more skilled or knowledgeable if they work hard and practice, it is more likely that your students will in fact learn more. For instance, it might be more educationally appropriate to give feedback such as "You must have worked very hard," rather than "You are so skilled."

Maslow's Hierarchy of Needs Theory

If you are an outdoor educator or aspiring to become one, you must familiarize yourself with Maslow's theory on human motivation. In 1954, the American psychologist Abraham Maslow fully developed his theory on human hierarchy of needs in his book entitled *Motivation and Personality*. Although Maslow's infamous theory is over 60 years old, his hierarchy remains a popular framework in management training, sport psychology, education, and especially outdoor education.

Maslow's Hierarchy of Needs is often portrayed in the shape of a pyramid with the largest, most fundamental needs at the bottom and the need for self-actualization and self-transcendence at the top. Yet, it is essential to understand that one cannot seek the higher level of needs without maintaining the fundamental one. Therefore, a more appropriate illustration of this hierarchy has been recently proposed. The figure below represents this new illustration of Maslow's theory.

Simply put, Maslow's theory suggests that the most basic level of needs (i.e., physiological, safety, love and belonging, and esteem) must be met before one can desire or be motivated to seek the higher level of need such as self-actualization.

Maslow acknowledged the likelihood that the different levels of needs could occur at any time in the human mind, but he focused on identifying the basic types of needs and the order in which they tend to be met, from basic or fundamental to self-actualization.

Because teaching in the outdoors involves teaching in a changing and uncontrollable environment often for long periods of time lasting multiple hours, days, weeks, or months, Maslow's hierarchy of needs is important to keep in mind as an outdoor educator. Learning can be impeded if the fundamental needs of students are not met.

Physiological and **safety** needs should be present before you aspire to build a sense of community or a positive self-esteem in your students. Consequently, your students might need to have a positive sense of **social belonging** and **esteem** before being able to **self-actualize** through learning new skills, knowledge or values.

In other words, before delivering your best Leave No Trace lesson, you might want to make sure that your students are warm, comfortable, not distracted by hunger or thirst, and generally feel good about their peers and themselves before exploring their own environmental ethic.

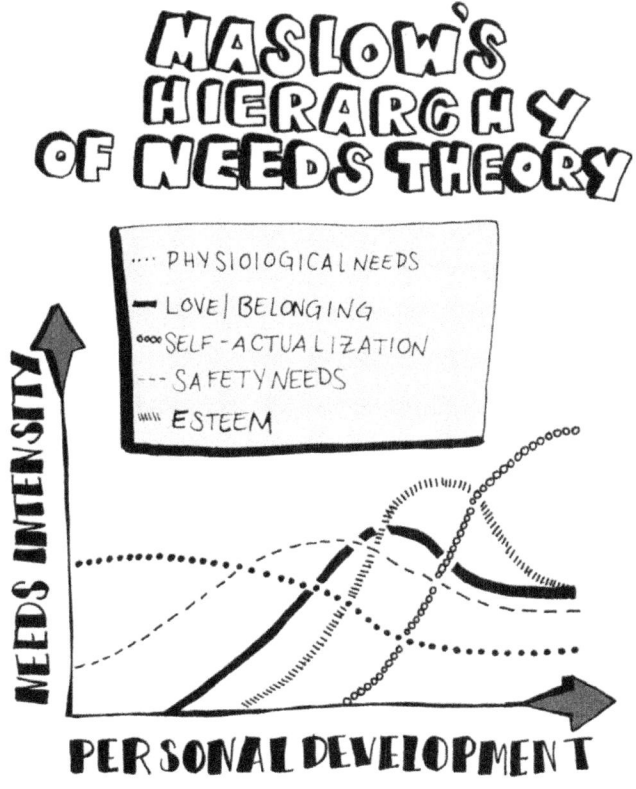

Maslow's Hierarchy of Needs Theory

Learning Models

Learning models can be defined as graphic representations of abstract ideas, concepts or theories. They are theoretical explanations of how people learn since "A picture is worth one thousand words." Familiarizing yourself with these models will hopefully influence your lesson planning and teaching in a positive way.

We have included the following learning and teaching models:
- Experiential Education Models
- Information Assimilation Model
- Gagné's Nine Events of Instruction Model
- Dale's Cone of Experience Model
- Teaching Strategy Level of Active Engagement Model

Experiential Education Models

The terms *Experiential Education* and *Experiential Learning* are now commonly used in education. Years ago, these terms were not mainstream, but today many schools or teachers proudly claim to offer an experiential curriculum or use an experiential approach in their teaching.

Of course, this powerful approach to teaching and learning is not limited to formal education. Today, experiential educators include outdoor educators, adventure educators, wilderness instructors, environmental educators, camp counselors, corporate team builders, therapists, challenge course instructors, outdoor guides, and more.

The Association for Experiential Education (AEE) has established a simplistic definition of experiential education. They define it as:

"Challenge and experience followed by reflection leading to learning and growth."

This simplistic and broad definition is useful as a tagline to explain experiential education to the general public, yet for professional educators like us, it is perhaps more meaningful to consider the extended version of AEE's definition of experiential education which reads as follows:

"Experiential education is a philosophy that informs many methodologies in which educators purposefully engage with learners in direct experience and focused reflection in order to increase knowledge, develop skills, clarify values, and develop people's capacity to contribute to their communities."

What we especially like about this extended definition is that it includes the possible learning outcomes of using experiential education. These outcomes: ***increase knowledge, develop skills***, and ***clarify values***, perfectly match the system we are using to categorize the various teaching strategies featured in this book.

AEE Principles of Experiential Education:

1. Experiential learning occurs when carefully chosen experiences are supported by reflection, critical analysis and synthesis.
2. Experiences are structured to require the learner to take initiative, make decisions and be accountable for results.
3. Throughout the experiential learning process, the learner is actively engaged in posing questions, investigating, experimenting, being curious, solving problems, assuming responsibility, being creative, and constructing meaning.
4. Learners are engaged intellectually, emotionally, socially, soulfully and/or physically. This involvement produces a perception that the learning task is authentic.
5. The results of the learning are personal and form the basis for future experience and learning.
6. Relationships are developed and nurtured: learner to self, learner to others and learner to the world at large.
7. The educator and learner may experience success, failure, adventure, risk-taking and uncertainty, because the outcomes of experience cannot totally be predicted.
8. Opportunities are nurtured for learners and educators to explore and examine their own values.
9. The educator's primary roles include setting suitable experiences, posing problems, setting boundaries, supporting learners, insuring physical and emotional safety, and facilitating the learning process.
10. The educator recognizes and encourages spontaneous opportunities for learning.
11. Educators strive to be aware of their biases, judgments and pre-conceptions, and how these influence the learner.
12. The design of the learning experience includes the possibility to learn from natural consequences, mistakes and successes.

Kolb's Experiential Learning Model

The most classic model representing teaching and learning experientially was proposed by Kolb in 1984. In the illustration below, we can see that experiential learning includes 4 phases: (1) **Concrete Experience**, (2) **Reflective Observation**, (3) **Abstract Conceptualization**, (4) **Active Experimentation**.

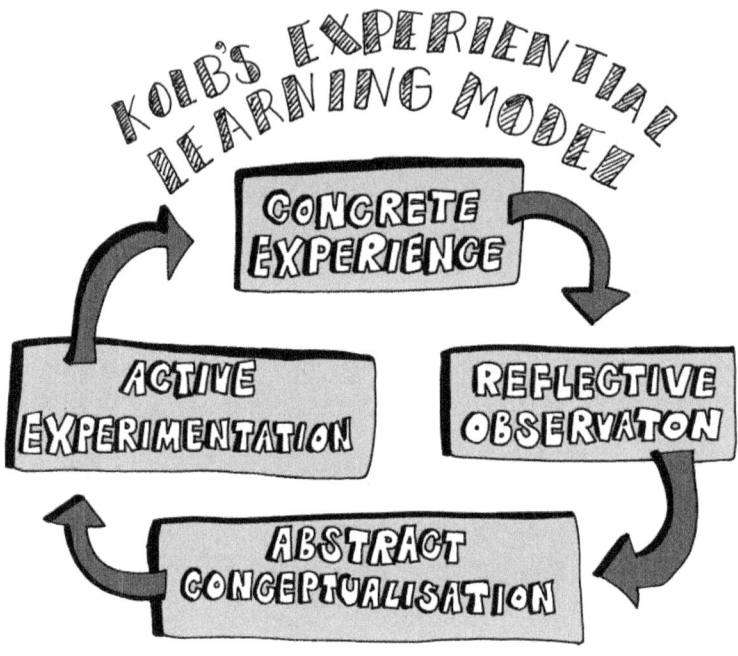

Kolb's Experiential Learning Model (1984)

Concrete Experience: The experiential learning cycle normally starts with a concrete experience. This is any activity that students can do without much prior instruction or direction beyond safety recommendations from an instructor.

Reflective Observation: In the second phase, students are invited to share their personal observations on their performance during the activity or any events or behavior they have observed within the group. This phase also includes actively processing the experience by identifying what was truly important or significant during the experience.

Abstract Conceptualization: In this phase, students are led through a facilitated reflection process to identify ideas or concepts which can be true in other situations.

Active Experimentation: The fourth phase of the cycle, often known as the "Application" of the learning, includes the transference and use of new concepts, behavior, attitudes, or skills to a new but similar situation.

Kolb's model is still referred in experiential education as a fundamental model explaining how people learn through experience and reflection, but it is also seen as simplistic. Many researchers and theorists in experiential outdoor adventure education have added new concepts to Kolb's model.

Priest's Experiential Learning and Judgement Paradigm Model

Priest (2005) proposed a 6-stage experiential learning and judgement paradigm model. In his model, Priest refines Kolb's model by sub-dividing the third and fourth phases. For Priest, the learning still starts with an (1) **Experience**, which can range from concrete and real to vicarious and theoretical. (2) **Induce**, during the post experience reflection, when students are invited to induce learning from the specific experience to general concepts. (3) **Generalize**, which represents the memorization of the new concepts into long-term memory. (4) **Deduce**, when students are asked to identify which general new concepts can be applied to a new situation. (5) **Apply**, the new concept to a new situation. (6) **Evaluate**, where students instinctively assess the success level of their application to the new situation.

Like Kolb's model, this 6-step model is cyclical, which means that your instruction can build from previous experiences along with the recent learning and reflection.

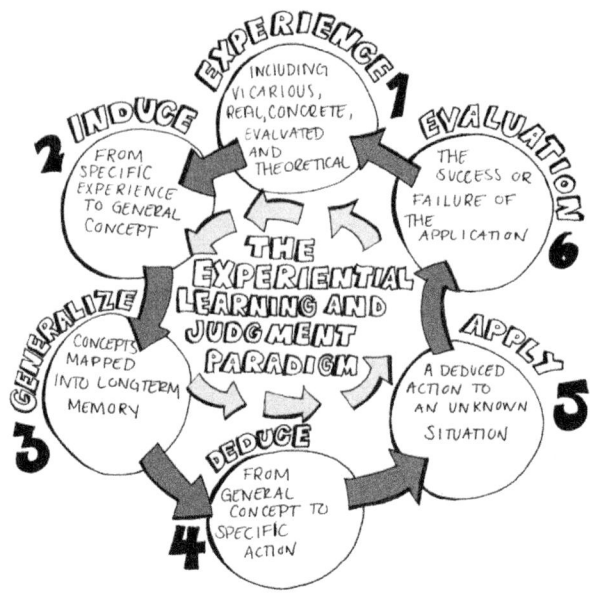

Priest's Experiential Learning and Judgement Paradigm Model (2005)
Model reproduced with the consent of the original author.

Priest and Gass 8-Stage Experiential Learning Model

Most recently, Priest and Gass (2018) have improved upon this last experiential education model by adding two new stages. By using a Möbius strip, they introduce an 8-stage experiential learning model which departs from the prevalent single loop models used to explain how people learn through experiences and reflection.

The new double loop model representing the experiential learning cycle includes the following steps: (1) **Experience**, (2) **Induce**, (3) **Generalize**, (4) **Memorize**, (5) **Deduce**, (6) **Apply**, (7) **Evaluate**, (8) **Modify**.

Note that in the first loop of the learning model, steps 1 to 4 correspond with the first three phases of Kolb's model (i.e., Experience, Reflection, and Conceptualization). The fourth step of the new model represents the inscription of the learning acquired through the experience and reflection steps. In the second loop, the new added step comes after the evaluation of the application of new newly memorized concepts. This 8th step, labeled as "modify," adds a second opportunity for the learners to improve on their application of new learning before restarting the double-looped experiential learning cycle.

Priest & Gass Double Loop of the Experiential Learning Cycle (2019)
Model reproduced with the consent of the original authors.

Theoretical models illustrating the experiential learning process will keep on being proposed and tested by scholars and experiential educators, but in the end, what is essential to understand is that a good lesson inside or outside the classroom should always include an experience and a reflection. So, if there is one model that should be on your mind when you are planning or delivering a lesson, it is perhaps the boiled down cyclical model illustrated below. "Experience and reflection," "hands-on and head-on," "action and theory," call it what you want, your students will always learn better if they are engaged in direct, meaningful, and relevant experiences with time to reflect and learn from these experiences.

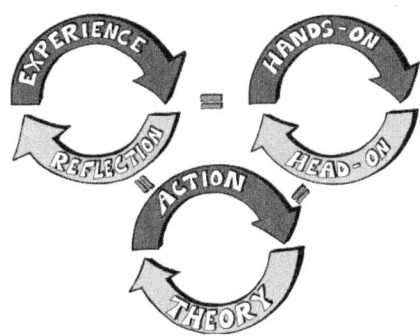

Information Assimilation Model

James Coleman (1976) contrasted the experiential learning method seen above with what he refers to as "Information Assimilation." For Coleman, information assimilation is representative of the dominant learning model found in most traditional classrooms. It is an approach to learning that relies heavily on the use of abstract symbols such as spoken or written words with some iconic symbols such as static or dynamic images (i.e., illustration or film/video). Think of the classic lecture in social science, health education, mathematics, language arts, or even the sciences; it is the classic classroom experience with no real-life application of the delivered content knowledge.

Priest and Gass (2018), illustrated Coleman's information assimilation with a 4-step sequential model. This traditional learning model shows students learning from structure to substance by experiencing the following steps: **Step 1** – students receive information about a general principle via symbols. **Step 2** – students are expected to assimilate and organize new information into a new set of knowledge. **Step 3** – students are expected to infer specific applications on their own from the general principles presented in the lesson, and finally, **Step 4** – when time allows or when a classroom teacher provides a concrete opportunity, the students are invited to apply and test the general principles which were the subject of the lesson. The information assimilation model is illustrated below with a corresponding example for each step when the topic for the lesson is CPR.

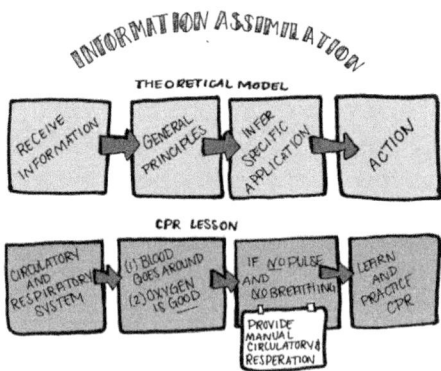

Coleman's Information Assimilation Model & Lesson Progression

You will notice that when the entire sequence in this learning model is completed, the lesson learned is quite effective and appropriate. After all, it would be appropriate to teach a CPR course by starting with some general principles (structure) before learning ways to apply these principles (substance).

In contrast, we have seen above that all current experiential learning models start the learning sequence with a direct, concrete and relevant experience, even if the experience is metaphorical in nature such as a challenge course curriculum. The model below, with a corresponding lesson on conflict resolution, represents the almost exact reverse sequence found in the information assimilation learning model.

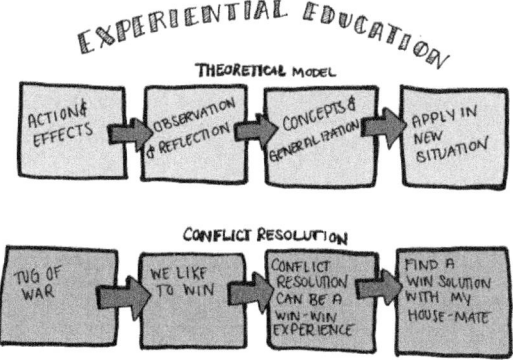

Experiential Learning Model & Lesson Progression

What is most important for you to remember is that information assimilation is not inferior to experiential education as a sequential learning method. It is often criticized because at times it is not fully completed. Because of time limitations, too often educators only apply the first three steps of the information assimilation model. This is when the learner asks the everlasting question: "Why am I learning this?" Without a concrete application, learning the general principles in any subject can be seen as futile and irrelevant.

Notice that the same can also be said for the experiential learning model if its sequence is not fully completed. Having an experience without a proper and appropriate phase for reflection might also feel useless and irrelevant, especially if the experience was metaphorical in nature. Who really cares if a student and her peers can help pass through a challenge course spider web?

Without a facilitated reflection, the true significance of the learning might remain hidden.

What is important for you to always know is which learning model you are using. Are you using an information assimilation or an experiential education approach? This knowledge will facilitate your lesson planning and delivery. Remember, both instructional approaches will be effective if you always give yourself enough time to either apply the general principles learned in a lesson trough information assimilation or discover the general principles and implications of an experiential lesson.

Gagné's Nine Events of Instruction Model

The figure below represents a model of Gagné's nine events of instruction highlighting its logical sequence and flexibility.

Gagne's Nine Events of Instruction Model

When using an information assimilation approach in your teaching, it could be more effective to follow Gagné's (1974) nine events of instruction. Although these nine events are meant to be flexible in their order, they represent a good instructional "architecture." It is a way to help your student's progress through the lesson in an organized, logical and effective manner.

Event 1: Gaining Attention: In this event, you will solicit attention from your participants by introducing the lesson with a "hook." A "hook" is a form of verbal or visual magnet which will bring students to attention and excite them for the upcoming lesson topic. A good hook could be a question such as: "Have you ever wondered how we could cross this river using ropes?" or "Does anyone here know what a Tyrolean Traverse is?" It could also be a fun *demonstration* via a short roleplay presented by the instructor(s). Imagine walking into an outdoor lesson site dressed up as old climber wearing wool nickers, long socks, nailed leather boots, a wool jacket and a great handle bar moustache. Rest assured, your students will quickly look at you with attentive eyes and smiles.

Note that gaining attention from a group at the beginning of a lesson is not the same as gathering a group for a new activity or sharing group-related information. The use of a hand signal such as "silent coyote" or a "Marco-Polo" like verbal commend such as "wolf – pack" are great examples of effective strategies to manage a group's attention and behavior in the outdoors. These techniques do not introduce your subject or excite the learners for the lesson they will soon be experiencing. We will cover these techniques more at length in chapter 2 under the section titled: Managing Groups Outdoors.

Event 2: Informing Learners of the Learning Objective for this Lesson: This event is self-explanatory and quite useful when included at the top of your lesson. Explaining at the beginning what skills, knowledge or values you anticipate your students will develop or explore is a good way to set the learning expectations for your students as well as for yourself. Take the time announce and perhaps write down on an outdoor teaching board these learning objectives so that everyone can be aware of them. On the flip side, allowing students to discover the challenge is also very effective.

Event 3: Stimulating Recall of Prior Relevant Learning: If your lesson topic is a continuation or building upon a previous lesson, it is perhaps good to quickly make reference to some of the important facts or concepts that were learned before. A good and engaging way to do this is by questioning your participants. Help them think about what they already know or experience since what you will now teach them will become more relevant if they see your lesson as a valuable addition to your previous lessons.

For instance, you can have a lesson on triangulation include a recall instructional event that will sound like this: "Remember when we learned to orient a map using a compass. What were the 5 essential steps to accomplishing this skill?" Invite them to collectively help each other identify these steps: (1) Set the compass dial at zero. (2) Identify the magnetic declination on the map of your current location. (3) Turn the compass dial to the proper declination angle. (4) Place the compass baseplate edge along one of the longitude margin lines. (5) Turn the map and compass as a whole unit until the magnetic red needle is in the orienting arrow "red in the shed." Then explain that learning triangulation will require them to initially use the same steps as orienting a map with a compass.

Event 4: Presenting New Learning Content: This is the core of your lesson. This is when you teach a new skill, content knowledge, or value using various teaching strategies that are featured in this book.

Event 5: Providing Learning Guidance: In this part of your instruction, it is sometimes appropriate to give "hints" or guidance on how to perform a new skill, apply a new knowledge, or think and reflect upon a value. Don't forget, your goal is to have your students be successful in their learning, so it is quite appropriate for you to share your tips or tricks as an expert.

For instance, you could share this canoe paddling technical tip with them: "Notice that when I steer my canoe in a side wind and my boat trim is heavier in the stern, I am more effective at performing my j-stroke when I paddle on the upwind or windward side of the canoe."

Event 6: Eliciting Performance through Practice: This event in your lesson will allow your students to practice their new acquired skills, content knowledge or value. This is when you will ask your students to perform a technical skill like tying a knot, give others feedback, or take on a leadership role. It could also be an opportunity for your students to apply some content knowledge such as identifying an animal track or predicting the possible weather for the next 12 hours by identifying the dominant wind direction and current cloud formations in the sky. Finally, it could also be an opportunity to ask your students to explore their own values by writing a short haiku describing their personality or debating what is essential or superficial when practicing leave no trace camping.

As you see, this event is crucial in making sure that theory and practice are present in your lesson. Without this instructional event, you are at risk of delivering an incomplete lesson as we explained in the information assimilation classic trap where a lesson only focuses on dumping information without application.

Event 7: Providing Feedback: If you are including Gagné's event number 6 in your lesson, then you can also include the next vital instructional event – feedback. Remember that most learners are starving for feedback on the application of a new skill, their understanding of new facts, concepts or theories, and your thoughts on a personal position (value) that they have on a topic or issue. Check chapter 5 to learn more about how to give effective feedback.

Event 8: Assessing the Performance: Once you have given feedback on a student's learning application, it is also important and essential for them to demonstrate the new learning again so that they can apply your feedback in their new performance.

For a technical skill, you can ask a participant to demonstrate their skill again while you assess their skill mastery. For content knowledge, after giving feedback on an incorrect answer to a question, you can ask them to rethink and reformulate their answer. Finally, for a value-based lesson, you can play "devil's advocate" and challenge their thinking, feeling, or opinion on a subject to see if they can produce a logical and coherent argument for their expressed value.

In education, we could say that assessment is often seen as the other side of the instructional coin. Therefore, a good lesson should always include some form of formal or informal assessment. Chapter 5 will look carefully at various ways to assess student learning.

Event 9: Enhancing Retention and Transfer to another Lesson or Life: The last event in Gagné's instructional sequence focuses on the transference of the learning to a future lesson or life itself. If it is appropriate and possible, this instruction event should match the last phase of all experiential learning models by focusing on the transfer of learning to new endeavors.

Education theorists and pedagogists like Gagné remind us that true learning is best proven when the learners is required to apply a new skill, knowledge, or value when confronted with a similar but quite different situation from which they have been exposed to during their learning exercise.

For instance, a lesson on decision making for outdoor leaders can be practiced using teaching strategies such as *role playing*, *case studies* and *simulations*, but the best way to test a young leaders' ability to make appropriate decisions is to have these leaders

	Instructional Event	Learner's Internal Mental Processes
1	Gaining attention	Stimuli activates receptors
2	Informing learners of the learning objectives	Creates level of expectation for learning
3	Stimulating recall of prior learning	Retrieval and activation of short-term memory
4	Presenting new learning content	Selective perception of content
5	Providing learning guidance	Encoding for storage long-term memory
6	Eliciting performance through practice	Responds to questions to enhance encoding and verification
7	Providing feedback	Reinforcement and assessment of correct performance
8	Assessing the performance	Retrieval and reinforcement of content as final evaluation
9	Enhancing retention and transfer to another lesson or life	Retrieval and generalization of learned skill, knowledge, or value to new situations

Gagné's Nine Events of Instruction Model Details

engaged in authentic leadership experiences in a different context with real consequences for both good and bad decisions. It is the ability of these young leaders to adapt to a new situation with new variables that will truly test them. This is where the leaning of new skills, knowledge or values, will be truly acquired by the learners.

Model Flexibility: These nine events are meant to be sequential in an ideal situation, but teaching is often an exercise in compromise, especially because of time limitations. Gagné emphasizes that his proposed nine events of instruction "should not be viewed as being invariably required for every lesson and learner." (Gagné, 1974, p.123).

As we will see in the next learning model, "time" for instruction is often the source of many instructional limitations and compromises. This is why some of Gagné's nine events of instruction can be bypassed, repeated, shortened or even delayed. Still these instructional events and their sequence can be seen as quite useful for any of your outdoor lessons since they have a positive effect on the learners' experience. The table below list the nine events and their corresponding effect on the learner's internal mental processes.

Dale's Cone of Experience Model

Dale's Cone of experience model is perhaps the most important learning model in this book because, as you will see in Chapter 4, the forty-two teaching strategies featured in this book are labelled according to their level of "experientiality." Edgar Dale (1969), like many other pedagogists and experiential education scholars, has argued that not every learning experience is equal, especially from the point of view of the learner's level of engagement.

In this book, the expression "level of active learner engagement" will refer to the amount and quality of engagement a learner will experience from the point of his or her various domains of self. These domains are: (1) Psychomotor, (2) Affective, and (3) Cognitive. You will notice that these three domains are borrowed from Bloom's domains of learning proposed in 1956 in his infamous text titled: *Taxonomy of Educational Objectives*.

By defining the level of engagement through these three domains, it supports the construct we are proposing in this book, which states that we can categorize every topic of instruction found in Outdoor Education into three big categories: (1) Skills – *Psychomotor*, (2) Content Knowledge – *Cognitive*, and (3) Values – *Affective*.

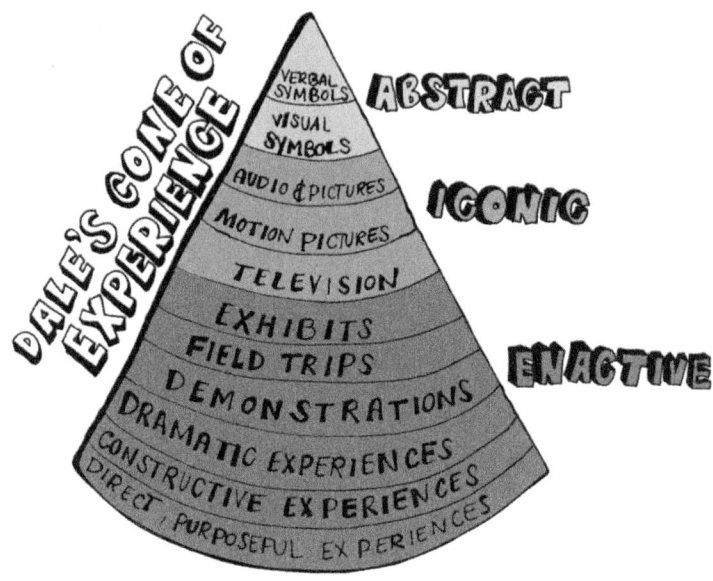

Dale's Cone of Experience Model

In 1969, Edgar Dale proposed a Cone of experience with eleven levels of learning experience ranging from "verbal symbols" (written words) to "direct purposeful experiences." In his model the more abstract form of learning experiences such as verbal symbols are located at the top or narrow end of the Cone, while the more concrete forms of learning experience, such as the direct purposeful experiences, are located at the bottom or wider base of the Cone. Although Dale recognized the limitation of using a cone as a visual analogy to the teaching and learning process, he attempted to represent the level of abstraction experienced by the learner by stacking the various and available learning experiences according to their level of "experientiality" or in other words, level of active engagement by the learner.

Dale saw three large categories of engagement, (1) symbolic, (2) iconic, and (3) enactive. The symbolic category includes highly abstract learning experiences such as reading a book or listening to a lecture from an instructor. The iconic category includes learning experiences using pictorial instructional tools such as written words on whiteboards, images, drawings, models, graphics, and video. The enactive category represents learning experiences with more direct involvement of the learner such as dramatization (i.e., *role-playing* and *skits*), contrive experiences (i.e., *simulations*) and of course, direct experiences.

We can also divide Dale's Cone of experience in two sections, the passive section which includes the symbolic and iconic categories, and the active section which includes the enactive category.

It is interesting to notice that although Dale was a pedagogist specializing in the use of audio-visual methods of instruction – a more passive iconic form of teaching – he recognized that direct experience was the ideal form of instruction and learning. He stated:

"The base of the Cone represents the concrete, direct, firsthand experiences that make up the foundation of our learning. Here are many of our richest, most vivid sense impressions – those that involve our feelings and perceptions in an eager exploration of the world. These lively, full-bodied occurrences are the bedrock of all education. Through seeing, hearing, tasting, feeling, and smelling – through the unabridged experiences of life – we build up our wealth of meaningful information and ideas." (Dale, 1969, p. 111).

Teaching Strategy Level of Active Engagement Model

It is from Dale's Cone of experience that we have developed our own learning model explaining the level of "experientiality" and learner's engagement found in the various teaching strategies featured in this book. Our new model features 8 levels of instruction. They are numbered 1 to 8 with the first three levels representing teaching strategies that present a more passive form of learning. Levels 4 to 8 represent teaching strategies that are more engaging. You will notice that some categories are found both above and below the line indicating the type of engagement (i.e., passive vs. active). For instance, you will find level 2 – Visual & Verbal the passive section of the model and Interactive Visual & Verbal in level 4 in the active section of the model because as you will see in the description of the teaching strategies at this level, verbal and visual based strategies of instructions can also be very engaging for the learners if delivered appropriately.

The same is true for some specific teaching strategies such as *Puppetry* which is found in level 3 when performed by the instructor team to an attentive but passive audience but also in level 6 as *Student Puppetry* when the learners themselves are performing the puppet show. See the table below to identify where each of the 42 teaching strategies featured in this book are found in the Teaching Strategy Level of Active Engagement Model.

Like any theoretical model, the **Teaching Strategy Level of Active Engagement Model** is not meant to be a perfect reflection of a hierarchy of teaching strategies from best to worst. It is simply trying to inform the teacher that in selecting different strategies, the experience of the students might differ in their level of engagement.

The model also presents a common reality when using more engaging or active forms of teaching strategies. This reality is often known as the "nemesis" of all dedicated experiential outdoor educators. The more experiential your lesson will be, the more time it might take to complete the lesson. For instance, it might take you 10 minutes to explain the importance of being known as a trustworthy person, but it might take you 30 minutes to engage your learners in a trust-oriented activity and process it to address the same "take home message."

So, if time allows for it, it might be better for your students to be actively engaged at a level 5 by performing a problem-solving activity than by being passively engaged at a level 1 when simply being told what they should learn about trustworthiness.

In Chapter 4 you will note that each teaching strategy is labelled according to its placement on the **Teaching Strategy Level of Active Engagement Model**. This will help you know how engaging, experiential, and time consuming the teaching strategy can be.

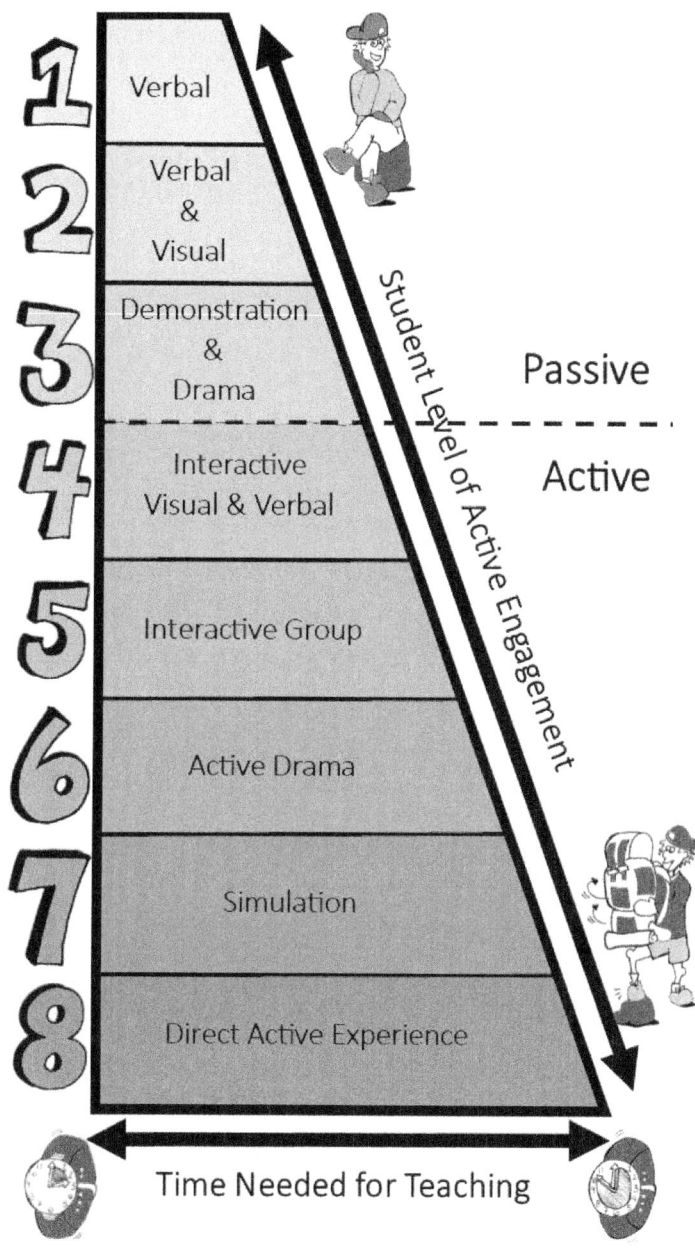

Teaching Strategy Level of Active Engagement Model

	Teaching Strategy Level of Active Engagement Model		
Level 1	Verbal	• Visual (Guided) Imagery • Quotes & Readings • Storytelling	Passive
Level 2	Visual & Verbal	• Video Feedback • Role Modeling	
Level 3	Demonstration & Drama	• Demonstration • Theatrics • Puppetry	
Level 4	Interactive Visual & Verbal	• Interactive Lecture • Lecture with Seeded Questions • Lecture with Seeded Facts • Lecture with Seeded Q-Cards • Mystery Challenge • Guided Discovery • Socratic Method	Active
Level 5	Interactive Group	• Case Studies • Student Storytelling • Discussion • Debate • Games • Problem Solving Activities • Group Journaling	
Level 6	Active Drama	• Student Puppetry • Skits • Role-Play	
Level 7	Simulation	• Simulation • Scale Modeling • Skill Modeling	
Level 8	Direct Active Experience	• EDP-ECP • Step-by-Step • Whole-Part-Whole • Physical Manipulation • Prompting Cues • Leap Frogging • Nature Awareness Activities • Art • Music • Personal Journaling • Exploratory Learning • Solo Experience • Peer Teaching • Service Learning	

Teaching Strategy Level of Active Engagement Model
With Corresponding Teaching Strategies

MYTH

WARNING: *If you search for models of Dale's Cone of Experience on the internet you will most likely find many adaptations of his original model as well as many models claiming that the model can express various levels learning retention. These models often propose percentages of learning retention ranging from 10% at the top of the model (Symbolic) to 90% at the bottom of the model (Enactive). All of these models are unproven and have actually been debunked by researchers such as Subramony et al (2014). So, do not fall into the trap of believing that because a lesson uses only verbal symbols (i.e., lecture) that knowledge cannot be acquired and retained by the learner.*

Adaptation of Dale's Model Proposing False Learning Retention

The Pedagogy of Fun

Fun is often not taken seriously, especially in education. Although most students like to have fun while learning new skills, knowledge or values, we too often think of the learning process as a solemn experience. While some view classroom education as a humorless environment, many people also perceive Outdoor Education as all fun and *games*. This perception is partially true; however, as you will see below, as outdoor educators we should not be ashamed of creating enjoyable learning environments.

Actually, we should be proud of using fun and engaging teaching strategies such as *games, simulations, role plays, skits, storytelling*, etc. in our outdoor lessons. However, we should also be able to justify our more playful teaching strategies. We should be able to explain that fun is not only an outcome of our teaching but often an essential part of our student learning. Do not promote "Edutainment" solely for its "entertainment" value, but because authentic learning can occur while being amused by the learning experience.

Therefore, if your personal style of instruction is leaning toward using fun as a pedagogical tool, rest assured that the process of having fun while learning (when appropriate) is totally justifiable. So, to build a better argument for an "Edutainment" approach to teaching, let us look at what essential characteristics define "fun" and how can it be used to enhance the learning process.

The two foremost and fundamental characteristics we can agree upon are that fun is "relative" and "situational." Basically, what is fun for one person might not be enjoyable for someone else and what we consider "funny" today might not be seen as "funny" tomorrow.

A third characteristic defining fun is that the feeling must be a voluntary experience. To experience fun, one must consciously or unconsciously accept, feel good, relax, let go, and let the situation be perceived as enjoyable. We all know from personal experience that fun cannot be forced or imposed upon someone. We can invite a person to join us in our play, but the final perception of enjoyment is left to the individual. In other words, it is not solely the experience that creates fun, an appropriate mental attitude is also imperative.

To use a *cliché,* we could say that "having fun" is a voluntary state of mind.

The last, but perhaps most important characteristic defining fun, is that our desire to "have fun" is inherent in our nature. Clinical psychologist, William Glasser has attributed so much importance to "fun" that he even considered it as one of human's five most essential needs: (1) the need to survive and to reproduce; (2) the need to belong and love; (3) the need to gain power; (4) the need to be free; (5) and the need to have fun.

These universal characteristics appear simplistic at first, but when we consider their pedagogical implications, we realize that they create an interesting puzzle for instructors. The problem they raise resides at a programmatic level. On one hand, we argue that fun is a natural emotion. On the other hand, we admit that because of the variabilities listed above, fun is difficult to predict and reproduce. Therefore, using fun in education becomes an uncertain science where the end results of our actions cannot be easily anticipated. So why would we want our students to have fun? Is it solely because it is in their nature, or are there other reasons to use fun in our teaching? Here are four reasons to make your students laugh.

1. Intrinsic Motivation

The most obvious pedagogical benefit associated with having fun is directly linked to the conditions characterizing its own occurrence. As previously mentioned, to experience enjoyment, one must first permit one's mind to perceive the situation as enjoyable. Consequently, this voluntary state of mind will provide a fertile ground in which intrinsic motivation, through enjoyment, will be allowed to grow. Research on the concept of fun/enjoyment directly connects intrinsic motivation with fun.

The role that fun plays with regard to intrinsic motivation in education is twofold. First, intrinsic motivation promotes the desire for recurrence of the experience. Secondly, fun can motivate learners to engage themselves in activities for which they have little or no previous experience. Fun can be introduced as a "No-Fault-Zone." Fun can allow learners to try new things without the fear of making a mistake, looking silly, or feeling awkward. With fun, new experiences, as strange as they may be, appear more inviting. Students will become motivated to participate in novel experiences or undertake new challenges.

2. Suspension of Social Reality

Another educational benefit associated with fun is the fact that when we are fully engaged in an experience and having fun, we momentarily lose our social inhibitions. Some professionals suggest that in actuality we are getting closer to who we really are; our true inner self. Through play, one can lose the notion of time, space, and most important, the notion of social barriers. As a catalyst, the combination of fun and play can eliminate inhibiting factors inherent to our socialization. In a sense, it is through fun that we can set free our inner self, try new things, trust others, and take emotional risks. By dropping these barriers, learners will be better disposed to face their own personality and evaluate their relationship with others.

3. Stress Reducer

Fun is also a stress-buster. Substantial researches in psychology and brain physiology have established the negative effect of harmful stress (i.e. distress) on the learning process. When the learner feels threatened physically or emotionally, downshifting becomes a viable response. Downshifting is one aspect of psychological distress and is defined by Caine and Caine as "a psycho physiological response to perceived threat accompanied by a sense of helplessness and lack of self-efficacy." When learners experience such a response, the learning process is jeopardized. On the other hand, a fun experience enables learners to change perceptions of "distress" into perceptions of "eustress" (i.e. a good form of stress). Hence, when fears and downshifting are absent, learning has a better chance of occurring.

4. Relaxed Alertness

Relaxed alertness is a combination of low threat and high challenge. These physical and psychological statuses represent the fourth benefit obtained through fun. According to the literature on brain-based learning, *simulations*, *games*, and the use of silly props are not just creating fun activities that make students feel good; they also help create an atmosphere, a feeling in which the learners are allowed to explore new possibilities. One of our goals as educators is to challenge learners discreetly and naturally so that new conceptual mapping (i.e. intellectual connections) will occur without engaging students into a downshifting response. Fun generates this no-fear or relaxed environment where learners feel safe to take risks, be creative, make mistakes, and most importantly, keep trying.

In the end, we can say with confidence that fun has a positive effect on the learning process. By inviting intrinsic motivation, suspending one's social reality, reducing stress, and creating a state of relaxed alertness, fun can be seen as a powerful teaching tool to enhance a motivating and safe learning environment. So remember, when you are teaching, don't be afraid to go for it. Have fun!

CHAPTER 2

Planning Your Teaching

Creating a Safe Learning Environment

Outdoor Teaching Considerations

Three Types of Lessons Taught Outdoors

Being a Reflective Teacher

Using Props & Visual Aids

Planning & Preparation

Creating a Safe Learning Environment

Setting a Positive Tone

Never underestimate the power of "tone." Whether you as an instructor intentionally or unintentionally set a course "tone," your students will absorb your words and actions and translate them into their view of the course or program ahead. The first hour you spend with your students is a golden opportunity for you to intentionally create a safe learning environment while setting a positive tone.

The tone you set should reflect the goals of the program but may also surprise you by transcending educational goals. A positive, safe learning environment is critical not only to the learning process, but also to interpersonal and intrapersonal health. When students feel physically and emotionally safe and supported, they are more likely to step out of their comfort zones, ready and willing to take on big challenges. When students do not feel safe and supported, they may hunker down in their comfort zone, scared of what lies ahead. It is your responsibility as an educator to create a space that feels so safe, so supportive, so inclusive and so encouraging, that students thrive on taking risks, challenging themselves and ultimately growing by leaps and bounds.

There are countless ways to create a safe atmosphere with your students. Since instructors hold the key to setting a successful tone, they can make or break a course by the tone they intentionally or unintentionally set. Tone begins the moment you meet your students, so it is helpful to start with a few fun activities that aren't too threatening to break the ice and encourage students to get to know one another. After beginning with a fun tone, you can move on to creating a safe atmosphere. Some literature in Adventure Education refers to this step as the Full Value Contract. There are many ways to set behavioral expectations while creating a safe, inclusive atmosphere. One approach that we have used quite successfully over the years, we call the "Safe Space Umbrella."

The Safe Space Umbrella

The "Safe Space Umbrella" is really a tool that gives students an opportunity to verbalize expectations of each other and expectations of the instructor(s). It also allows the instructors to spell out expectations they have for the students on a course.

In groups of three or four, give students a sheet of paper and have them brainstorm a list of all of the expectations they have for each other during the course. Next, have the students make a list of all the expectations they have for their instructor(s). On a dry erase board or mylar sheet pulled over a ground pad, draw a metaphorical umbrella that symbolizes the safe learning environment or "Safe Space." You can also use an actual umbrella and attach tape or labels to it. Put three headings in columns under the umbrella:

Your expectations of each other
Your expectations of the instructor(s)
Instructor expectations of you

Have the small groups come together and share their expectations with each other as you write them on the sheet under the first heading. Then have the students share their expectations of you, the instructor as you write these under the second heading.

Finally, it's your turn. If you set your students up well for this activity by frontloading the importance of identifying sincere expectations, they will have already laid out all, or almost all of your expectations for them. Draw an arrow from their "expectations of each other" column to the last column "Instructor expectations of you." You can do the same for the column listing student expectations of the instructor. The students will quickly find that the expectations are similar. Now add any expectations that you have for the students that they did not identify. This is a critical piece. Creating your expectation list in front of the students gives you a perfect opportunity to set very clear expectations of what is included under the "course umbrella." This is where you set the tone. Here you can also establish priorities such as safety of the individual, care of the environment, care of the equipment, etc.

Elements helpful for setting a safe, positive tone:
Fun
Growth Mindset
Positive & motivated instructors
Expectations clarified
Emotional safety addressed
Inclusive environment addressed
Physical safety addressed
Course goals established
Individual goals established
Honesty emphasized
Respect emphasized

After setting a supportive, inclusive tone by clarifying expectations and setting priorities, it is important to move to the next level by emphasizing that from this point forward, you are all under this umbrella together. You are all working to help each other stay safe from storms that go on outside of the umbrella. The umbrella is our safety zone. Everyone is important. Everyone is respected. Only positive energy is welcome. Spell it out clearly and emphasize zero tolerance for emotional or physical unsafe behavior. Be specific. You are a team now. You are all interconnected in a positive way. There is no room for sarcasm or put-downs because they inevitably lead to negative downward spirals.

It is also extremely important to note that instructors are expected to adhere to all of these expectations just as the students are expected to adhere to them. No exceptions. If instructors slide, the integrity of the safe umbrella crumbles and the safe, positive tone that you initially created will fail.

Explain that each member of the team is now responsible for holding others accountable to the "code." Use whatever teaching style works for you, but in the end, be serious. You have hopefully already played with the group and demonstrated a fun, lively tone, but now is the time for emphasizing the importance of your expectations. If you are too lighthearted about expectations, students may think it is a game. They may even think that you will not really hold them accountable for their behavior. Drive it home so that there are no questions in the end about what is OK behavior and what is not OK behavior.

Try to avoid:

Avoid singling out a student negatively

Avoid using inappropriate or negative humor

Avoid being non-inclusive

Avoid swearing and using negative sarcasm

Avoid having favorites and double standards

Outdoor Teaching Considerations

Nature provides the greatest classrooms on earth. Outdoor classrooms are unique, real, and direct, connecting students with the land and the topics they are learning. That said, Mother Nature might easily throw a handful of surprises or challenges at you and your students that could definitely hinder the learning process if you are not prepared. As an instructor, it is important to be aware of site safety, environmental factors and human factors when teaching outdoors.

Site Safety

Before ever beginning a lesson outdoors, always assess the terrain in advance and make sure it is safe for your group. If you are near the base of a climb site teaching movement on rock, is your group situated safely so that they are clear of potential rock-fall? If you are at the top of a climb site teaching top-rope anchor set-up, did you set-up very clear boundaries in advance? It is critical to minimize risk where possible and manage risk where it is an unavoidable part of the learning process.

Environmental Factors

Some environmental factors that your group may face include weather, sunlight, slope, loud noise, water, and darkness. When preparing your "classroom," take into account the direction your students will be facing. Position yourself so that you are looking into the sun while your students have their backs to it. If appropriate, try removing your sunglasses and wearing a hat or visor so that students can see your eyes when you teach. Our eyes tell a lot through expression. If they are covered, students may miss your subtleties.

An ideal site may offer students a chance to sit on a slope or position themselves in a circle so that they can see and hear you and each other better. If it is really hot, make sure that you are teaching in the shade. Heat can be incredibly uncomfortable and therefore distracting. In these situations, emphasize drinking water during class. If the wind is intense, try to find a sheltered classroom tucked behind rocks or trees. If it is cold, make sure students come to class with warm clothing and a ground pad to sit on if needed. In some situations, encouraging students to have a hot drink in hand also really helps with comfort and motivation!

Another element to consider is noise level. If you are teaching a river crossing class right next to a large river, students may not hear you very well. In this situation, you could begin your class back from the river while you teach a few key parts to your lesson and then move closer to the river for the parts of the class that really need to be near or in the water. Also be aware of student voices. Find a site where students asking questions can be heard by everyone or repeat questions as needed. If the location doesn't allow for students to hear you and each other, find a more ideal spot before you begin your class.

In situations where students will be getting wet for class, take into consideration the temperature of the air and water and the length of time that students will be wet. Learning starts to decline quickly when students can no longer focus due to cold and wet conditions. Having dry clothing nearby and a thermos or stove on hand is a good idea.

During the winter and shoulder seasons, a lot of teaching outdoors is done in the dark. Some teaching strategies, such as *storytelling*, lend themselves extremely well to being taught in the dark with or without a single light glowing. Other classes require pre-planning on your part for students to see and interact in the dark. Lanterns work great if you are base camping or traveling with sleds. If you are going light, placing a few headlamps by water bottles or having a couple of students shine a light on the instructor works just as well.

> **Teaching Tip**
>
> If you are teaching in rainy or snowy conditions, it is helpful to have a tarp or two set up over your classroom. When the weather doesn't cooperate, it can be fun for students to huddle up under a tarp and learn something new.
>
> You can also use tents. One effective way to teach in lousy weather is to make stations. If you have two or three instructors, each one can take a topic, teach it under a tarp or tent, and then rotate to other tents while the students stay warm, cozy and dry. Students love this, and instructors can fill an afternoon of cold rain with an hour or two of productive teaching, skill practice, *storytelling*, etc. These

Human Factors

Before deciding to teach a lesson, assess your student's physical and emotional state. Energy levels are affected by altitude, weather, sleep, nutrition, bodily functions, and exercise. Students who are new to outdoor experiences may initially find it more physically challenging than you would expect.

It is a good idea to observe and check-in with your students to make sure that their physical needs are being met (Maslow's Hierarchy of Needs). Are students tired, hungry, or thirsty? If so, give them a break! Let students take care of themselves first before they feel pushed into learning something that they may not be ready for. There are obviously situations where you may need to teach a technical skill to a tired and hungry group just to get them quickly and safely through a specific type of terrain, but more times than not, when you plan ahead, you are able to avoid these tough teaching situations.

> **Teaching Tip**
> If you are camping in places where your instructional site is far from student tents, then when students get into camp, consider having them create a camp pack to organize their gear in an accessible manner. This goes a long way in setting them up for successful learning.

> **A Camp Pack could include the following:**
> Headlamp
> Water bottle
> Bag of food
> Raingear
> Warm layers

In addition to physical needs, it is important to make sure your student's emotional needs are being met. Is someone nervous or scared? Is the group as a whole feeling burnt out? Keep up with the pulse of your group before trying to teach them anything. As an instructor, you could teach the best lesson in the world, but if your students aren't comfortable, hydrated, and well fed, or if they are nervous or don't feel safe, do not expect them to learn or retain much.

Beyond teachable moments, successfully teaching outdoors often comes down to stellar planning and preparation. If you find a safe site and prepare yourself and your students well for dealing with human and environmental elements, you will set everyone up for success in learning.

> **Additional seasonal and site-specific items:**
> Ground pad or camp chair
> Warm upper and lower layers
> Warm hat & gloves
> Mosquito net & sunscreen

Managing Groups Outdoors

Group Management Considerations Common to All Settings

Establish expectations upfront.

It is helpful if you are clear about how you expect students to act when you speak to the group. Do you want everyone's full attention or are side conversations ok? Can students get up and leave your class randomly when they want to move or go to the bathroom without communicating with you? Do you have signals? Is it ok for side conversations to go on while you are speaking? A lot of your expectations may vary depending upon the situation, the group, and the type of class, but being clear with yourself and then with your students will help eliminate frustration on both ends.

Consider the physical arrangement (proxemics) of how the group is positioned around you.

Can all of your students see and hear you? Is everyone included in part of the group circle? Are some "double parked" behind other students? Are some far out of the ideal teaching/learning zone? As an instructor it's important that you help guide group arrangement since students rarely go naturally into "perfect" formation for the type of class you are teaching. Frontloading how to position themselves (standing, sitting, moving, etc.) and where to position themselves (in a circle, line, small group, with partners, etc.) while you teach will set everyone up for optimal learning.

Consider the comfort of the group.

Are your students dressed appropriately for the environmental conditions or prepared with spare layers (raingear, jacket, hat, mittens, etc.)? Are they sitting on the cold ground or do they have pads to sit on? Are they well fed? Do they have water bottles with them or nearby if they get thirsty? Are they positioned in the sun or shade? Managing the comfort of your group upfront with clear expectations will help prevent discomfort and interruptions in your lessons. Having a daypack with comfort essentials that everyone is expected to bring to lessons may help diminish interruptions.

Consider the maturity of the group.

Younger students often need more guidance than older students, but specific group dynamics also may affect how you manage your group. Are there any students who tend to distract each other who are planning to sit or work together? At times it can be helpful to casually point to a spot and ask a student to move there while the group is arranging themselves. Every instructor has their own style or way of doing this depending upon their rapport with the group. You can do this in a joking but intentional way, a gentle reminder way, or a direct and matter-of-fact kind of way. It all depends on you, your group and the situation. Remember that for optimal learning to occur, students should really want to be there. They need to know that you genuinely care about them and their learning.

Consider additional group management situations that are site specific.

There are many different settings to consider when managing groups outdoors. Establishing management strategies for different settings will ensure smoother transitions and help contribute to a safer learning environment.

Outdoor Front Country Established Classroom Management

Seating
Is there enough space for the size of the group? Is there established seating that is optimal for the type of lesson that you are about to teach, or do you need to move out of the established classroom?

Weather
Is there a rain/sun/snow cover on your classroom? What is the sun doing during the time slot that you will be teaching? Is it shining in student eyes? Wind! Is the wind going to blow away all of your props? Will students be able to keep hold of their lesson materials? Is the weather conducive to teaching an effective lesson outdoors or is it one of those days that students will learn better inside? This is the front country after all. Use good judgement. You don't need to prove anything by having your students suffer when a better learning environment is nearby. Change plans when needed.

Bugs

Are they manageable? Are students prepared for black flies, mosquitoes, or ticks with head-nets or bug spray? Many incredible lessons can be lost to student negative preoccupation with bugs. Once again, in the front country you have a choice. Be wise and move your group if necessary, otherwise group management may be very difficult.

Outdoor Front Country Non-established (Wild) Classroom Management

Safety

Establish boundaries early! Formal outdoor classrooms typically have boundaries. Non-established outdoor classrooms typically do not. When you settle on an outdoor space to teach your group, be clear about where students can go. This is especially important with younger students. If you have a lesson that includes moving around an outdoor "classroom" and exploring different areas, be sure to set clear physical boundaries upfront. It is also very helpful to have a specific call or signal when you want to regroup with your students.

To manage large groups of younger students, try assigning each student a number and practicing a "count off" so that you can count students when you regroup. This also works when traveling back and forth to outdoor classrooms. It's also important to establish what students can do in the wild. Can they climb trees or boulders? If so, how high? Thinking through these types of scenarios will help you anticipate the complexities of managing students outdoors.

Seating

In forest "classrooms" with no formal seating or classroom structure, consider managing your group upfront before anyone positions themselves. It typically helps if you place yourself first and then ask students to arrange themselves according to your guidance. If there is a comfortable looking rock or stump outside of your optimal teaching zone that you anticipate everyone rushing to sit on, place something such as a pack on it to ward off the temptation. If you want everyone to spread out and find a special tree to sit by, make sure that there are enough nearby trees within your optimal teaching zone.

Weather & Bugs

See the section above. These strategies apply to established and non-established front country classroom sites.

Backcountry Campsite Group Management

Safety

Setting up safety expectations upfront can help avoid unsafe behavior. Upon finding and establishing camp, it is helpful meet with your group to establish boundaries. With younger groups especially, it is important to lay out very specific boundaries at every campsite (such as the creek or the large boulder by the edge of the kitchen, etc.). More mature groups usually do fine if you work together to establish camp "boundary" principles during the first 72 hours of your course. As long as students know the expectations for where to go to the bathroom, where to set up kitchens, where to not wander alone, etc., they should be able to stay within reasonable proximity without specific landmarks.

OUTDOOR EDUCATION TEACHING STRATEGIES

Activity Specific Safety Protocols

When in camp, students need to know upfront if they are allowed to wander down to a lake and just jump into water alone or if there are safety guidelines around swimming (which is likely). If you are in a rock camp, is there a limit on bouldering? Knowing your organizational safety protocols and procedures as well as how to manage unanticipated hazards around campsites is critical in safely managing groups in backcountry campsites.

A great way to manage campsite safety is by grouping up your students not long after getting into camp and discussing, showing, and possibly even demonstrating what is safe and acceptable and why. Include your students in explaining why. Sharing thoughts on what is not acceptable and why can be really helpful in some situations.

Animal Awareness/Safety

Black bears, grizzlies, moose, mountain lions, snakes and more have been known to wander into camps. Making sure to teach your students how to prevent encounters in camp and what to do if they have an animal encounter in camp is critical very early in the course.

Regulations

Different land management agencies have different regulations for camping. Knowing these regulations and managing your student behavior by teaching them the rules will help ensure that you and your group don't violate guidelines.

Group Management Tips for Regrouping

There are hundreds of ways to call your group together for instruction. Classroom teachers do this all day long. Choosing strategies that work for you and your students in different settings is key to being physically safe, emotionally safe, and highly efficient.

Establishing Regrouping Expectations

Be very clear with your students about what you expect of them when you group up together. This is extremely situational and often age dependent. Do you expect everyone to look at you and stop talking? Do you expect students to wander over at their leisure?

Whatever the norms are that you decide to establish with your students, you need to be consistent with expectations or regroupings could become frustrating for both parties.

Regrouping when scattered:
Send a runner with a meeting time and place.

Regrouping when nearby:
Code Words: If you are within verbal distance, you could yell a code word that means "come now as quickly as possible and make a circle while standing quietly ready for instructions." Students have more buy-in if you work together with them to come up with their own special word. Compound words work great for this strategy. For example, you yell WOLF and students immediately know that this is their cue to yell PACK (Wolfpack). To speed regrouping along with younger students it helps to give a countdown (10, 9, 8, 7, 6, 5, 4, 3, 2, 1).

Action/Reaction Words: There are some classic environmental education strategies that work incredibly well while traveling or hanging in camp. Yell these words out just for crazy fun or to regroup enough to talk to everyone or start a lesson. These examples are forest specific, but the principle can be adapted to any setting.
"FLASHFLOOD!" At this cue, students know that they have 10 seconds to climb up on a log, tree, rock or anything outside that gets them a few inches off of the ground. This also moves along quicker when you apply a countdown. Adults love this too, but don't necessarily need a countdown.
"MOOSETACHE!" At this cue, students run and grab a stick off of the ground or a pinecone, leaf, rock, etc. and place it on their face like a mustache. Many students are even able to hold it in place without hands, using just their nose and face muscles. This is funny and it brings everyone together.
"ANTLER!" Students race to pick up two sticks and place them on their head like antlers while grouping up so that everyone can see. This works especially well with "Moosestache."

Regrouping Scenarios
Different scenarios require different strategies for regrouping. Below are a few strategies that may give you some ideas.

Regrouping scenario: yell out "moosetache" and count to ten as your students come together to show their moosetaches. Many talented students can hold sticks up on their face up by simply puckering their lips! This typically gets a laugh out of all ages.

More Regrouping Scenarios

Sounds: There are endless ways to grab a group's attention by playing with sound in the midst of a lot of noise and activity.

Clap once and say, "If you can hear me clap once." Sometimes nothing happens. Sometimes a few people hear and listen. Then Clap twice and say, "If you can hear me clap twice." Usually a few more join in. Then clap three times and say, "If you can hear me clap three times." Depending on the size of the group (this can work well with huge groups), before you clap five times everyone is usually clapping with you. End by saying, "If you can hear me sit quietly and wait for instructions." This is a classic and effective method.

Clap a rhythm with your hands and pound a rhythm with your feet. Ask the group to echo your rhythm. Then improvise and have the group echo. After you teach your group this, anytime you create a rhythm, they know to echo it. It immediately stops activity and gets a group ready to listen.

Non-Verbal Signals: Any positive hand signals can work to get a group focused for listening. It is similar to a code word, except it is not spoken.

Put your hand straight up in the air and wait for others to do the same. It can take a while to get everyone's attention using this technique because it only works if you are observant.

Put your hand up in a "quiet coyote" shape with your middle finger touching your thumb and your other fingers in the air. This is also a classic environmental education and classroom technique.

Three Types of Lessons Taught Outdoors

What is learning? The late outdoor educator Clifford Knapp once wrote: "Learning is the process of acquiring and constructing knowledge." (Knapp, 1993, p.25) Although this is a commonly accepted definition of the term "learning," and with great respect to one of our mentors - Dr. Knapp, we would like to propose two additional common outcomes of the learning process. We propose that during an outdoor lesson, the learner can also acquire "skills" and "values."

Skill	Definition	Examples
Physical / Technical	Gross and fine motor skills as well as practical skills.	Teaching how to lift a backpack (Gross Motor Skill). Teaching how to tie a figure eight on a bight (Fine Motor Skill). Teaching how to light a white gas stove (Practical Skill).
Interpersonal	Skills which relate to the interactions between one another.	Teaching how to give feedback. Teaching how to communicate effectively. Teaching how to display trustworthy behavior.
Intrapersonal	Skills or attributes which relate to oneself.	Teaching how to make decisions as a leader. Teaching how to display grit amidst adversity. Teaching how to reflect on one's behavior.

We can approach the planning of any outdoor lesson by knowing that the lesson we are about to teach will either focus on the development, reinforcement, or acquisition of skills, knowledge, or values, or a combination of any of these three lesson outcomes.

An understanding of these three possible lesson topics is essential since, as you will see in this book, different teaching strategies are more suitable for teaching different types of lessons. Each teaching strategy described in this book is grouped into one of four categories: (1) Skill oriented teaching strategies, (2) Knowledge oriented teaching strategies, (3) Value oriented teaching strategies, and (4) Multi oriented teaching strategies.

To effectively teach a technical skill such as tying a bowline knot, it would be more appropriate to use a teaching strategy such as Explain-Demonstrate-Practice, Evaluate-Correct-Practice (a.k.a. *EDP-ECP*). However, using *EDP-ECP* to teach about cloud families and cloud types would not be appropriate or even remotely effective since the topic of the lesson is not a technical skill but rather content knowledge.

Knowledge	Definition	Examples
Facts	Information that is considered to be true or objective.	Teaching the elements of the Wilderness Act of 1964. Teaching the origin of the name of a flower such as a Dandelion. Teaching about the components of the GPS system.
Concepts	An abstract or generic idea generalized from a reality.	Teaching the reason behind the proper physical position of a belayer in relationship to a top rope anchor. Teaching the importance of proper blood perfusion in the human body during a vascular injury. Teaching the importance of speed, angle, and lean downstream (SAL) to take an eddy turn in a kayak.
Theories	The general or abstract principles of a body of facts in science, social science, humanities or the arts.	Teaching about plant succession in an aging forest. Teaching about the impact of climate change on wildlife habitat and distribution. Teaching about the heuristic traps leaders can fall in when making a decision.

Content-knowledge oriented lesson topics such as cloud families and cloud types would be better instructed via a teaching strategy such as an interactive or seeded lecture supported by visual aids. When it comes to values, it is more effective to use a teaching strategy such as *personal journaling* or a *solo* when the topic of the lesson is the Human-Nature relationship.

Values	Definition	Examples
Personal	The general expression of what is most important to a person.	Exploring one's position regarding social justice. Exploring one's feelings about risk taking. Exploring one's commitment to group success.
Social	The general expression of what is most important for a group, community, or society.	Exploring the importance of trustworthiness in friendship. Exploring the impact of gossiping on group cohesion. Defining the acceptable behavioral norms for a group.
Environmental	The general expression of what is most important for one in regard to the natural environment.	Exploring one's carbon footprint on the environment. Defining one's personal relationship with Nature. Exploring the role of modern society on the planet's climate.

In our teaching experience, we have also discovered that many teaching strategies are suitable for more than one lesson topic. For example, *puppetry* can be used to teach content knowledge — meaning some cool facts — about an animal such as a beaver. Yet, using a beaver puppet can also be helpful in teaching about values such as land ethics. Imagine using a beaver puppet to explain the tension between a nature-centric and an anthropocentric view of the world when it comes to the question "should we or should we not destroy a beaver dam?"

Being a Reflective Teacher

Honestly, the best teachers are reflective teachers. Since teaching is a complex experience involving the whole person, from cognitive to affective and psychomotor, it's vital to reflect on what we do as teachers since so much of oneself is poured into this activity.

There are two principle channels for you to be a reflective teacher. First, you can and most likely will reflect on your teaching after completing a lesson – let's call this form of reflection the "off-line channel." The second channel will also be experienced naturally. It is found in our ability to think on our toes, to reflect in the moment. Let's call this form of reflection the "on-line channel."

Off-line Channel

There are many ways for you to reflect on your teaching after delivering a lesson. You can keep a teaching journal and write your impressions of your teaching by answering questions such as:

Were students engaged?
What activity worked in this lesson?
How were my transitions between activities or experiences?
What should / could I change the next time I teach this lesson?

Another important off-line strategy for reflection is to share with a colleague how your lesson went. Explain what you did, highlight your success, share your concerns, and carefully listen for feedback from your colleagues along with your own thoughts. Remember, reflecting through the off-line channel often brings clarity to your teaching performance. As the popular idiom says: Hindsight is always 20/20.

Since the term "reflection" can also mean to project a mirror image of an object, you should consider using technology to capture images of your own teaching. Using a video camera with a good microphone will give you an objective reality about your own instructional skills. Reviewing your teaching video off-line can give you the opportunity to truly access your teaching mechanics such as your voice projection, voice cadence, body language, facial expression, eye contact with your students, and more. Read the section on "Teaching Mechanics" later in this chapter for more tips.

On-line Channel

Reflective teachers often have an inner voice while teaching a lesson. This inner voice might be asking: "Is the lesson working?" "Are my students learning?" "What else should I be doing?" This is when reflection is happening live during the act of teaching. It is happening through your on-line channel.

On-line reflection often yields the best ideas for a lesson. When you are engrossed in the act of teaching, you can simultaneously teach and think about your teaching. When you achieve this state of thinking-in-action, you open yourself up to being more flexible in your instruction, changing your lesson sequence or activities based on influential factors such as changes in the outdoor environment, the learners' response to your instruction, or time remaining for the lesson.

This ability to "think on your feet" while instructing can often open up your creativity as a teacher. Don't forget that as we mentioned earlier in this book: teaching is a science and an art, so don't be afraid to be creative and follow your instinct while teaching. Take chances with your lesson plan, don't feel like you need to follow your plan to the letter. Be open to new ideas. If it works – great! If it does not, you can always reflect on why it did not work during your post lesson reflection.

Using Props and Visual Aids to Enhance Learning

Students have the capacity to comprehend lessons much more effectively when multiple domains are involved. When students actively participate in experiences that utilize their senses, they are more likely to retain the information learned because their brain becomes more engaged. Combining effective visual aids or props with oral delivery inevitably helps most students comprehend your lessons on a much deeper level.

Visual aids and props can take on infinitely different forms. Although outlines on ground pads or dry-erase sheets have their place, challenge yourself to be imaginative and engaging. Using natural materials such as snow, sand, trees, rocks, mountains, students, instructors or yourself, can go a long way in creating novel learning moments that are truly memorable. Natural prop making materials are usually quite abundant, you just have to be creative and open to challenging yourself to try new things.

Imagine drawing the key points of a "movement on rock" class on your body to help students visualize "power" coming from their legs while their hands act as "hooks." Or demonstrating the difference between a static rope and a dynamic rope by hanging one mini "banana dude" from a cotton string and one from an elastic string to show what happens to each banana dude during a lead fall. During a first-aid class try using colorful markers to outline a real backbone and spinal column on a student, or, during a leadership class, have students identify the qualities of a positive leader by writing qualities on athletic tape and taping the qualities onto a volunteer "Leader."

Building a three-dimensional mountain out of snow or sand and making contour lines on it with string or dye is a classic approach to helping students transfer a three-dimensional shape to a two-dimensional image for practicing map reading skills. Teaching glaciology with a cirque in the background offers an ideal visual aid that you can refer to while immersing students in their surroundings. These are just a handful of ideas to spur your imagination. Risk being creative and finding out what works for you and your students.

If you need to carry a prop into the backcountry, try to make it as lightweight as possible. Using an inflatable globe to teach latitude and longitude or weather patterns is definitely worth its weight. It also doubles as a prop for teambuilding activities. Small hand puppets or toys can also go a long way in helping to teach anything from natural history to social skills.

Making props from materials that you are already carrying into the field simply requires you to think outside of the box to see how versatile your supplies can actually be. Raincoats, sleeping bags, stuff sacks, canoe or kayak hulls, trowels, spice kits and pots all have abundant prop potential. A permanent marker can turn most normal items into super star props. Turning spice bottles into mini-figures by drawing eyes and wild hair on them can help animate and reinforce key points about a lesson you are teaching. Using a black sleeping bag placed over an instructor serves as a great black bear costume for demonstrating what to do if you encounter a bear. The sky is the limit and your gear has unlimited prop potential. Once again, you just have to be creative.

It is important to note that as much as effective props and visual aids can help your students process information on a deeper level, ineffective props and visual aids can actually distract immensely from the learning experience. If your prop is boring, poorly made, or distracting, it will defeat its purpose, leaving students confused and unsure of your intent. If your prop is so funny that students actually miss the message, then you need to make sure that you clarify things or use a different approach. Planning ahead, challenging yourself to think through ways to really deepen student learning, and then actually preparing your class thoroughly, will help ensure that your visual aids and props are truly meaningful.

Teaching Mechanics

As mentioned earlier, teaching is a science and an art. In addition to on-line reflection and action, the art of teaching also includes the physical performance of the instructor. Imagine teaching as equivalent to a stage performance. Actors and stage performers have to use two main tools to deliver their art. These tools are their voices (verbal delivery), and their bodies (physical delivery).

The presentation of a lesson through verbal and physical delivery is called teaching mechanics. These mechanics are essential for the effective delivery of any skill, content knowledge or value-based lessons. Effective communication is a cornerstone of the teaching profession, therefore developing good teaching mechanics is essential for your success as an outdoor teacher and also for the success of your students. Remember, students are always more engaged in a lesson when it is presented by an effective communicator with good verbal and non-verbal communication skills. If you don't feel like this is your strong point, remember, these skills **can** be learned!

Verbal Delivery

The primary source of most communication is verbal delivery. It is through your voice that you will mainly connect with your students. It is through your verbal delivery that you will inform, direct, correct, motivate, and organize your students. Therefore, using an effective voice while teaching, especially when teaching outdoors, is a key component of delivering an effective lesson. Speech mechanics relevant to teaching that you will want to consider are listed below:

Voice Projection

What is the volume of your voice? Can everyone in your group hear you, or are you yelling when teaching? Projecting your voice is not the same as yelling. If you are teaching outdoors, remember that natural noises such as wind, river, waterfall, and other ambient noises can cover your speech. Like a stage actor or an opera singer, to project your voice, you will need to learn to use your diaphragm to project your voice without becoming an intimidating instructor.

Voice Tone

Your tone of voice is affected by your emotions. It is your tone of voice that indicates what you are feeling and what level of energy you are presenting when teaching. It is also a subtle expression of what you want your students to feel. If you want them to be excited about their next learning activity, your tone of voice will need to express excitement. If you want your students to be reflective for the next few minutes, your tone of voice will need to express calmness. Your tone of voice can convey intangibles such as professionalism, a caring attitude, passion, respect, and many other important values.

Voice Clarity

Voice clarity refers to pronunciation, word quality and articulation. Basically, does your speech include clear and distinctive word production? In normal situations, it may, but be careful that under the stress of teaching, you maintain this clarity. A fun self-test for voice clarity is to recite a classic English language tongue twister such as: *"She sells sea-shells on the sea-shore. The shells she sells are sea-shells, I'm sure."*

Cadence

Cadence of speech refers to the speed of your verbal presentation. The classic mistake here is to speak too fast when you get nervous or feel rushed to get a lesson taught in a certain amount of time. There is no specific number of words per minute to have a good cadence but keeping your pace understandable is obviously important.

Punctuation

No one likes listening to an instructor with a monotone voice. This is why punctuation is an important element of speech mechanics. Proper punctuation allows you to accentuate or emphasize the important points you want to teach. It allows you to highlight what is really critical to know. In addition, variety in your speech will keep your students engaged in your lesson. Remember

Verbal... "Um" ...Fillers

In casual speech most of us use "verbal filler" words in order to fill the silence while we are trying to think of a word, an expression, or our next sentence. As a result, we use sounds and words which are common, but distracting in an instructional speech. These filler words include, but are not limited to:

Um (and its variants, such as "uh" and "eh" if you are Canadian)

Like, Kinda, sorta, and, you know, hmmmm, so....

Solutions:

Adopt a new attitude toward periods of silence in your verbal delivery. Be comfortable with silence, use pauses in your speech to your advantage. Become aware of your verbal filler(s). Use a video recording of your lesson to identify your filler or fillers and look for them creeping out in your next lesson. Once you are aware of them, you can start controlling and eliminating them.

Learn to breathe during your verbal delivery. Use the natural pauses in your verbal delivery to take the time to take a conscious breath, calm yourself, and focus your thought on your next sentence.

If needed, practice your verbal delivery by replacing your natural verbal filler with the word "pause" spoken out loud. After a few practices, practice your delivery by internally saying the word "pause".

that pausing and having some silence in your speech can help students identify important "take home messages" in your instruction.

Vocabulary

In terms of speech mechanics, vocabulary is not a classic element of effective speech, but it is very important for you as an outdoor educator. The choice of words you use in your instruction can inform, clarify, and simplify your message, or it can confuse or even turn off some of your learners. Your choice of words during instruction should always be professional and appropriate for the maturity level of the learner. It should also be respectful, culturally sensitive and gender sensitive. Avoid exclusive language including undefined acronyms or technical lingo. Don't assume that everyone knows what "LNT" or "on-side" paddling means. Finally, be consistent with your vocabulary, use and reuse the same technical word throughout your lesson to avoid confusion.

Physical Delivery

The secondary source of communication is physical delivery. Although typically it supplements your verbal communication, non-verbal communication is also critical since it will be captured by your learners at a conscious and unconscious level. Your instructional physical delivery can support and enhance your verbal delivery therefore it is an element of your teaching mechanics that deserves attention. The physical mechanics relevant to teaching that you will want to consider are listed below:

Eye Contact

Making eye contact with your students will help them feel engaged in your speech, as if you are talking to them personally. Therefore, as mentioned earlier, it is important to place your group and yourself in an arrangement which will allow you to easily make eye contact with each of your student (proxemics). Be careful of students positioned on the fringe of your peripheral vision. If needed, reposition them or yourself before starting your lesson. When teaching, take the time to scan your group to make eye contact with your students. Be careful not to focus too much on one specific student unless you are interacting with this specific student during the lesson.

Body Gestures

Your communication will be reinforced by your overall hand and body movements. Be aware of the subtle message your gestures can transmit. For instance, pointing a finger to address a student is often perceived as an act of aggression while placing your hands palms up in front of your body while saying, "What do you think?" shows openness for input from your students.

Body Posture

Pay attention to your overall body posture when teaching. Does your body posture show confidence, respect, approachability and a caring attitude, or does it show nervousness, fear or boredom? For instance, having your hands in your pockets might indicate calmness and confidence before engaging the group in a risky activity, but it can also indicate detachment and a lack of interest when teaching a lesson topic for which you should display excitement and enthusiasm.

Facial Expressions

There are 43 individual muscles in the human face. These muscles are responsible for a multitude of macro and micro expressions which express our emotions when communicating. Be aware that your students will pick-up clues from your facial expressions. These facial clues can express positive emotions such as confidence, respect, a caring attitude, excitement, or passion just to name a few. The same can be said for a long list of negative emotions. So, be aware that your facial expressions can enhance or derail your teaching.

Getting Started: Planning and Preparation

Teaching is exhilarating, exciting and incredibly fun! It offers immeasurable rewards and challenges and can impact students for years to come. However, keep in mind that teaching is not necessarily easy. You must plan, prepare, deliver, observe, adapt, assess, and reflect upon your teaching. It is an art, a science and more. The beauty of teaching is that although you as a teacher can always improve through life-long learning, you also have the potential to master this art by planning ahead and using creative teaching strategies that best suit your students, your environment, your time slot, and your topics. Here are some tips to help get you started.

Planning

Know your material. Whether you are teaching a physical skill, content knowledge or value-laden topic, it is critical to know your subject well since access to extra information is not typically possible in the woods. This point cannot be emphasized enough. It is also important to know your students. The best lesson may flop if it is taught at the wrong time or to the wrong population. Later, you will see a chapter dedicated to knowing your students because it is such a critical part of planning your lesson.

Lesson Plans

In terms of teaching tools, a lesson plan is an incredibly valuable tool for preparing a new class. If you have never taught a specific topic, creating a lesson plan will serve as a valuable guideline to help you organize your thoughts while making sure you have all of the information needed to cover your topic thoroughly. The actual act of creating the lesson plan can help you identify goals, objectives and details. The plan itself can serve as a tool for reviewing your lesson before you teach, like a blueprint, so you can verify that there are no holes in your progression.

After teaching the lesson, in order to make improvements for the future, it helps to reflect "off-line" and re-visit the lesson plan while making any changes that you think will improve the lesson before you teach it again. Usually, after teaching a lesson a few times and reflecting and refining your lesson plan, you will not need to rely on this written tool as much since it will gradually become etched into your brain. Even if you do not find yourself using a written lesson plan over time, it is still quite important to continually improve your teaching by trying new strategies or variations on methods that you have been using. Always adapt the lesson to your group and seek updated information on your topic to keep your skill level and knowledge base current. Life-long learning and reflecting is one of the pieces that makes teaching so fun!

Components of an Effective Lesson Plan:

Part I: Planning and Preparation

Educational Goals: State the purpose for teaching the lesson, such as "This lesson will help students learn how to build an effective shelter using a tarp."

Educational Objectives: Objectives are specific, measurable and observable outcomes of your lesson. For example, "The learner will be able to effectively build an A-frame shelter using a tarp and two trees."

Student Background Knowledge: Determine what your students should already know and verify that they know it before you teach this lesson. For example, "the students should have already learned the trucker's hitch and bowline and know how to carefully select an appropriate campsite."

Location: Scout and describe a safe, preferred location for this lesson such as "an open forested area." Also have an alternative location for bad weather such as "a more sheltered location if it is really windy."

Materials: A list of all the materials you will need to teach this lesson. For example, "3 tarps fully equipped with cordelettes, 24 tent pegs."

Length: The estimated time you think it will take to complete the lesson.

Part II – Lesson Content and Methods: What will you teach and how will you teach it.

Opening: The opening, also known as the "hook," is designed to begin your class by grabbing your student's attention and motivating them to learn more. It is intended to be a short, fun way to ignite your student's interest in learning.

Body of Instruction: This should be a sequential outline of the lesson, including the content you are covering and the teaching strategies you will be using to deliver the lesson. You may also want to describe your visual aids or props and explain how they will enrich the lesson. This section should be detailed enough that another competent instructor could teach this lesson using only your lesson plan. (See Appendix for sample lesson plans).

Part III – Evaluation and Closure

Evaluation: Determine how your students will demonstrate that they met the lesson objectives. Will you pose questions, lead a *discussion*, stage small group challenges, hold practice demonstrations, or play a game such as "Tarp Olympics?"

Closure: Wrap-up your lesson by emphasizing key points and answering any questions the group has. It is also effective to end on a fun, positive and encouraging note. Depending upon the type of lesson that you are teaching, you can then help the group generalize main points and transfer the learning to other situations.

> **Tip - Using Outlines**
> It can be helpful to have a quick bulleted outline of your less to use when teaching. A quick outline will help trigger your memory while you are teaching. It is basically a "cheat sheet," but that is absolutely OK, especially when you are new to teaching, teaching a topic that is new to you, or teaching something that you haven't taught for a long time.

Preparation

After making a solid plan, make sure that you have all of the resources needed to teach the class well. Scout your teaching site in advance and gather the necessary materials. If the topic is new to you, don't be afraid to "practice" teaching. Most good teaching is very intentional. After considering everything needed get started, it's time to deliver!

CHAPTER 3

Teaching Outdoor Expedition-based Experiences

Grasshopper Approach

Planning the First 72 Hours

Length of a Lesson

Using Teachable Moments

The Grasshopper Approach to Curriculum Planning

In his book, *The New Wilderness Handbook*, Paul Petzoldt (1984) introduced a curriculum planning approach specific to wilderness-based educational expeditions. This approach is known as the **Grasshopper Method**. Although Petzoldt introduces the grasshopper as a way to teach in the out-of-doors, it is not a teaching strategy but really a method to plan a series of lessons throughout a wilderness expedition. In other words, it is a good way to plan your curriculum.

The grasshopper analogy is appropriate here since like the insect, you will want to "graze" at your entire curriculum throughout the length of the expedition. And, like the grasshopper, traveling the landscape to find a better feeding ground, you will wait for the best venues to teach certain lessons as your travel along your route. This is why planning your route in conjunction with your instructional curriculum objectives is so important when working as a wilderness educator.

As you will see later in this chapter, the first three days (72 hours) are often used to teach lessons that are essential for the wellbeing and safety of students. They are the lesson topics that are often labelled as "need to know". But the grasshopper curriculum planning goes be beyond the first 72 hours. It includes planning for the entire expedition and including more "need to know" and "nice to know" lesson topics.

After the first 72 hours, you will want to plan lessons in a thoughtful sequence which will factor the special activities required in your expedition such as off-trail navigation, a nature *solo experience*, or a small group hike without instructors. Your grasshopper planning will also factor in the location, environment, and specific landscape you will encounter throughout your route such as major river crossing, alpine zones, portages, habituated bear areas, lightning prone areas, etc.

A good example of using the grasshopper curriculum planning method is when thinking about the progression you could use when teaching portaging. For instance, the following progression for this topic could go as follows on a 14-day canoe-camping expedition:

Day 1: Teach a basic two-person hand-carry to move a canoe to and from the waterline.

Day 4: The lake route you are traveling brings you to a long and very narrow sandy peninsula. Since you have noticed on your map that the narrowest part of the peninsula is most likely free of vegetation and only about 60 feet wide, you plan to teach a canoe group carry to hop quickly over the obstacle at that location.

Day 6: On this day, your route brings you to your first real portage, about 500 feet long or 30 rods in the Boundary Waters of Minnesota. Therefore, on this day you plan time to teach the two-person canoe carry. You teach that a good strategy for this short portage is to carry the canoe first, then return to get the rest of your equipment.

Day 8: Your route brings you to a longer portage, ¼ mile long or 80 rods; this is the best time for you to teach the single person canoe carry with a spotter. You teach students how each canoe partner can take turns portaging the canoe using the yoke while the other walks in front of the canoe carrying canoe packs and paddles.

Day 12: Your route finally brings you to the longest portage of your canoe route. A mostly flat forested portage of 1 mile long or 320 rods. For this significant challenge, you teach a new portage strategy including two stages. In the first stage, the canoe is carried by one person all the way to the end portage. You instruct how to look for natural features along the trail (i.e., low sturdy branches, down trees high across the trail, trees forming a "V", or large rocks) to safely rest the canoe and take breaks. While the other canoe partner hikes to the halfway point of the portage and drops the first load of equipment. In the second stage of the portage, the paddler who portages the canoe can return to the middle of the halfway point and pick-up the equipment and portage it to the end of the portage, while the second partner returns to the beginning of the portage to pick up the rest of the equipment and portage it all the way through the end of trail. This way, each canoe partner has to carry a load for only 1.5 miles instead of 2 miles.

As you can see, the grasshopper approach to curriculum planning can be carefully matched to a progressive sequence of instruction for many topics which are best introduced at the right time and place during a wilderness expedition. Remember, the goal of the grasshopper method is to present lessons in a sequential way according to their relevance based on the route or the special event planned for the expedition.

Planning the First 72 Hours

There is an immense amount of teaching that takes place during the first 72 hours of a backcountry course. Thoughtful, upfront planning will help ensure that you cover all of these essentials in a fun, effective and efficient way.

Teaching priorities within the first three days of your contact with students often focuses on the following five categories: Safety, food, shelter, travel, and hygiene. The order and priority of your lessons within these categories typically depend upon the logistics, course type, environment, student age, skill level, and behavior, program goals and most importantly, time. Below is a sample 3-day curriculum plan for a summer and shoulder season northeast backpacking course.

Safety
- Community Building
- Trip overview
- Expectations
- Proper equipment (clothing, gear)
- Group gear
- Staying found
- Water purification
- Animal safety
- Lightning safety

Food
- Identifying & packing food
- Stove use & safety
- Cooking
- Kitchen clean-up/sanitation/LNT
- Hanging food/using canisters

Travel
- Backpack packing
- Hot spot & blister prevention
- Pack adjusting

- Basic contour map reading
- Navigation plans
- Pacing & breaks
- Dressing appropriately
- LNT on the trail

Shelter
- Campsite selection
- Shelter set up
- Sleeping comfortably
- Weather & animal proofing
- LNT in camp
- Packing up camp

Hygiene
- LNT Cat holes
- Disinfecting
- Female & male specific hygiene
- Brushing teeth

Length of a Lesson

Time is not always on your side. Even on a multiple week expedition, finding time to fit everything in that you want to teach can still be a challenge. You have to account for the fact that students aren't always in a learning mode. They also need to live, travel, reflect and enjoy themselves!

Prioritizing lessons is helpful in planning and implementing your curriculum. Thinking about what students must know and what is nice to know for the type of course that you are leading is a great place to start.

After laying out your first 72-hour curriculum plan, consider what will be essential to teach students during the length of your course. Other than covering course critical safety lessons, your "must know" classes will often be program, location and student dependent. The same holds for classes that are "nice to know." For example, a geology class can be nice to know, but it may not be essential unless your program is focused on natural history. Keeping these two categories in mind should make prioritizing easier while easing your time crunch.

Time

Time limitations and situations may force you to teach something very quickly with students as passive learners. On your first day out if a lightning storm moves in, you will need to quickly stop and teach students what to do to be safe. Since time isn't on your side, a quick 5-minute lecture or *demonstration* will suffice. In this situation, the teaching strategy is less experiential with students as passive learners because there is simply not time to get them actively learning all of the ins and outs of lightning before the situation gets unsafe. If you have to teach a quick lesson, later teach a thorough lesson with high student engagement when you have more time.

Honestly, there is no reason other than a time crunch for you to just lecture to passive students. When time is on your side, challenging yourself to teach using strategies that highly engage students will lead to more fun and effective learning. Students love to be involved! It's how they learn best.

Using Teachable Moments

If you instruct outdoors, teachable moments surround you! Identifying a teachable moment is really about being aware of your physical surroundings and your group. Deciding whether or not it is the right time to throw in a teachable moment is key. Focusing on special natural history tidbits, physical skills, or ethical issues at opportune times can provide powerful learning opportunities.

Different strategies can be applied to different types of teachable moments depending upon your learning goals. If you are rigging a bear hang system with students and they show interest in learning more knots, perhaps try teaching knot tying using a *step by step* strategy. If you are backpacking with students and come across bedrock with multiple dikes, you could teach some geology content through questioning or guided discovery. If your group watches an amazing sunset together after climbing all day at Cochise Stronghold, you could read a quote or excerpt that highlights the Native American struggle on that land while later asking students to share thoughts that highlight their values.

If your group is struggling to make unified decisions, you could stop everything and set-up a problem-solving challenge that forces them to work together. Better yet, you could maximize your unique environment and utilize an authentic problem-solving challenge such as asking the group to figure out how to set-up a bear hang when there are no trees with big branches or asking small groups to rig a tarp that keeps out horizontal snow or rain.

Direct instructor feedback is critical in completing this type of instruction. Being observant and aware of your surroundings, your group needs, and potential authentic group challenges is a major component of pulling off a successful teachable moment.

Something to be aware of is avoiding the pitfall of overusing or misusing teachable moments. If you stop too often to use teachable moments, if your group needs to travel far, or if your students are hungry and trying to get to camp before dark, it isn't typically helpful to present a teachable moment. The engagement level and effectiveness will be very low if Maslow's Hierarchy of Needs takes over.

Experienced instructors often have plenty of material in their head to spontaneously present a teachable moment. However, it is also effective to approach a teachable moment as an amateur. You don't have to be a specialist in everything, you just have to have some resources and enthusiasm for learning new things. If you come upon a new plant that you know nothing about, instead of passing it by, you could get excited about how unique it is and look into guidebooks for more information about this beautiful flower. You may find out that it is edible! *Role modeling* a passion for learning is highly infectious. If you are genuinely interested in learning, your students will inevitably catch the bug and want to learn too!

CHAPTER 4

Teaching Strategies

Teaching Styles vs. Teaching Strategies

Skill Oriented Teaching Strategies

Knowledge Oriented Teaching Strategies

Value Oriented Teaching Strategies

Multi Oriented Teaching Strategies

Teaching Styles vs. Teaching Strategies

This chapter presents 42 distinct teaching strategies that can be used to teach skill, content knowledge, or value-based lessons. Some of you might wonder, "Why present so many different teaching strategies?" Well, the simplest answer is that like a good carpenter, a good teacher should be able to use many tools to build an effective curriculum. The more teaching strategies you have in your "repertoire of instruction" the more options you will have to deliver your lessons. Plus, it is important to realize that some lesson topics are better taught and learned when using certain teaching strategies. Hopefully these 42 strategies will launch you into seeking out or creating even more strategies for teaching creatively.

Therefore, not only should you have a large selection of teaching strategies in your "teaching tool bag," you should also learn to become more astute in the art of selecting the appropriate teaching strategy. This skill will come through practice but also through the understanding of certain influential factors such as (1) logistics (time frame, time of the day, preparation time available, and equipment available); (2) curriculum (subject being taught and educational goals) and (3) social (group maturity and group energy). These factors will be further explained throughout this chapter.

Factor's influencing teaching strategy selection

Logistics
Time frame
Time of day
Preparation time
Equipment available

Curriculum
Subject being taught
Educational goals

Social
Group maturity
Group energy

Teaching Style vs. Teaching Strategies

Before introducing the various teaching strategies used in outdoor education, it is important to differentiate teaching styles from teaching strategies. Too often the terms are interchangeably used in outdoor education literature which can lead to confusion. As you will discover in this text, the term "strategy" will define a method or technique of teaching that has a sequence of events and specific actions, along with interactions between learners and teachers, learners and the subject or between learners themselves.

Meanwhile, for the purpose of this text, the word "style" will be used to describe the particular manner in which someone teaches. It is important to remember that teaching is an interpersonal activity; therefore, one's personality will define one's teaching style since it is impossible to teach without expressing one's own persona. For instance, if your personality is fun and lively, your style of teaching will reflect these characteristics. If you are more reserved as a person your teaching might be more formal. If you are a detail- oriented type of person, you might like to share many facts with your students.

What is most important is that your teaching style is true to your personality. If you are attempting to be someone else while teaching, your students will see through it. Students will respond more favorably to an authentic teacher than to someone who is attempting to mimic another's style of instruction. Never forget that teaching is based on trust between the instructor and the learners. Therefore, to be considered trustworthy, a teacher's voice, demeanor, and interaction with the students must be genuine.

However, there are some personality traits that are best avoided. Teaching with a sarcastic, rude, divisive, or a patronizing tone of voice will not create a healthy teacher – student relationship. Using off-color jokes or foul language to elicit an easy laugh can be offensive. Remember that you are responsible for creating a safe learning environment for all of your students. The tone you set via an exercise such as the "Safe Space Umbrella," described in chapter 2, must be supported by your own actions throughout your teaching. As we will see later in this chapter, teaching through *role modeling* can have a very positive effect on your students. Therefore, it is essential that you develop a teaching style that reflects the best side of your personality.

Skill Oriented Teaching Strategies

EDP - ECP

Step by Step

Whole - Part - Whole

Physical Manipulation

Prompting Cues

Video Feedback

EDP - ECP
Skill Oriented Teaching Strategy

Explain, Demonstrate, Practice
Evaluate, Correct, Practice

When describing how to teach technical skills, Paul Petzoldt (1984) often summarized a basic teaching strategy by using the phrase: "Describe, Demonstrate, Do." This method, known as the 3-D's was fundamental for teaching many technical outdoor skills such as knot tying, shelter set-up, cooking, or how to use a compass. Today, outdoor instructors know that the process of effectively teaching a skill includes a few more elements and does not limit itself to gross or fine motor skills.

Explanation and Demonstration

This strategy begins with a careful verbal description of the skill before performing the skill or while simultaneously performing a *demonstration*. If a skill requires speed or continuous motion to be completed, such as a Telemark ski turn or an Eskimo role, the description can come before or after a full *demonstration*. If the skill does not require you to perform a fluid action, then the verbal description can be presented while you are performing a skill *demonstration*. For instance, when teaching how to tie a bowline knot, you can carefully describe the components and sequence of action while tying the knot. In either situation, remember to always ensure that your students are positioned in a way that will allow them to easily see your *demonstration* and hear your explanation. In addition, make sure that your verbal description is clear, simple and not overloaded with unnecessary details. Also, ensure that your students are not distracted by trying to copy your movement because they are holding the same equipment you have. If you want them to carefully pay attention to your *demonstration*, you might need to ask them to put away their gear so they can focus only on your visual and verbal instruction first.

Practice

A skill cannot be acquired if it is not practiced. Therefore, one of the most important elements of this teaching strategy is to allow ample time for your students to practice the skill. This will require you to solve logistic issues prior to your lesson to assure an effective skill practice period during your lesson. This means that you will need to assure that you have enough equipment for all the learners or at least pairs of students before presenting your lesson.

There is nothing more frustrating for you and your students than to teach a technical skill lesson with limited equipment. Imagine trying to teach how to take a field bearing with a compass to 12 students using only two compasses. The end result is that your lesson will take much longer than necessary and will not provide what educators call a quality "time on task." Time on task is the concept that basically says, to acquire a technical skill during a lesson, one must spend a maximum of quality time practicing the skill during a lesson. The same compass lesson taught with 12 compasses or at least 6 – where students could work in pairs to practice the skill – would greatly improve the "time on task" factor of the lesson.

EDP
Explain
Demonstrate
Practice

ECP
Explain
Correct
Practice

Yet, spending time on developing a new skill can be frustrating and pointless if it is not practiced with quality. As the new axiom says, "practice makes perfect but perfect practice brings mastery." One can easily spend lots of time practicing a skill that only reinforces poor habits. Therefore, to assure quality, the instructor must provide not only the right amount of equipment but also the proper gear in the proper context or environment.

For instance, when teaching climbing anchor systems, it would be more effective and transferable if an instructor provided each student or small group of students with a full climbing rack and access to vertical cracks at the base of a rock wall. In this learning environment, students will be able to safely practice a new skill in a concrete and authentic context.

Evaluate and Correct

During the practice period, the role of the instructor is to observe the performance of the learners and provide feedback when appropriate. Here are some tips on how to give effective feedback during this phase of the *EDP-ECP*. First, make sure that your feedback is specific. Saying "Good Work Jaylen" might help the affective domain of the learner but will provide little to no information about the skill itself. In contrast, saying "Jaylen, the catching and power phase of your forward stroke is really effective. Your paddle shaft is almost vertical when the blade enters the water and you stop your power phase at your hip – nice effort!" With specific feedback the learner receives valuable information that helps them develop skill mastery.

The same principle can apply to constructive feedback. For instance, following the previous example, the instructor could also say, "Jaylen, I see you are putting a lot of effort into this stroke. Notice the recovery phase of your forward stroke. It could be improved if you assure that your blade is feathering like the wing of a bird through the air. This will save you energy on long paddling days." Again, we can see here that being specific in your feedback will enhance your students' learning. Emphasizing effort will also help your students maintain a growth mindset.

Second, the feedback should be timely – meaning that your feedback should come during or right after the performance of the student. Delaying a specific feedback will make it irrelevant. An effective feedback like, "Ami, I noticed this morning during our anchor building lesson that you were very focused and engaged. This is a good way to acquire these skills, please, keep up the effort!" This type of feedback can be effective even if it is shared a few hours after the event and again during a check-in session with a student, but skill-related feedback should be offered as closely as possible to the skill performance.

Finally, feedback can be individual or collective, but one should not replace the other. Individual feedback is given to a specific student, while collective feedback is given to a small or entire group of students. If you notice an error in someone's performance, use individual feedback. If the error is common to many or all students, then stop the entire group and share your feedback or re-teach the skill if necessary. Try to avoid giving a group feedback for and isolated problem with one student's performance. It will only do two things, (1) confuse the rest of the group and (2) possibly embarrass the student who has difficulty with the skill.

Practice (again)

After giving feedback, it is essential to encourage students to perform the skill again. This is when you will be able to assess if the students were able to incorporate your feedback into their performance. This is also when you will notice that some students are acquiring the skill at different rates. Some will already know how to perform the skill, some will acquire the new skill rapidly, while some will struggle. In these instances, you might need to use different levels of challenge. While you are spending time helping students who are struggling with a new skill, you can keep more advanced students engaged in their learning by giving them new and more difficult conditions to perform the skill. It might mean asking a student that is proficient doing a J-stroke on the right to perform it on the left, or a student proficient at tying a figure 8 to do the same knot with their eyes closed. You could also give students who are proficient in a skill a leadership challenge by asking them to help others or do some *peer teaching*. The goal here is to keep every learner properly challenged and engaged.

During the practice period of this teaching strategy, you might observe that it may be difficult to keep students engaged in practicing a new skill. Often students will interpret your request to practice a skill as a request to perform the skill only once. Therefore, be very specific in your expectations. Ask students to perform a skill a certain number of times, such as 30 repetitions, or for a certain length of time, such as for the next 10 minutes or until "I tell you to stop". Without these expectations, you will often see students getting off task after only one or two attempts at practicing a new skill.

Skills Taught Through EDP-ECP

Too often instructors assume that the *EDP-ECP* teaching strategy can be used only to instruct gross and fine motor skills such as rolling a kayak or tying a knot. In reality, *EDP-ECP* can also be used to teach interpersonal skills such as giving feedback, resolving conflict, or active listening. The same teaching strategy used to teach a climbing move can be used to teach your students on how to give feedback. Imagine explaining the important points regarding how to give constructive feedback, demonstrating it, then asking your students to practice the skill in pairs. While they are practicing, you are walking around the group listening to their feedback, making corrections when needed, and then encouraging them to continue their practice. Although the skill sets presented above are very different from motor skills, students learning social or communication skills can also benefit from the same teaching strategy.

Example: Tying a Bowline Knot

Imagine a situation in which you are planning to teach a shelter set-up class later, but first your students need to know how to tie a few basic camping knots. You decide to teach them the bowline knot. After getting enough nylon cord for everyone to practice, ask them to sit in a tight circle for your lesson. The lesson could go as follows:

Ask your students to hold their rope with their right or left hand, whichever they prefer. Then ask them to do exactly what you do – after a short pause, release your grip on the rope and let it drop to the ground. Ask your students to leave their rope on the ground and pay close attention to your **explanation** and **demonstration**.

After explaining the properties of the bowline and the rational and contexts for which the knot can be used, **demonstrate** how to tie the knot by **verbalizing** each step of the knot.

Before letting students practice you may decide to redo the *demonstration* of the knot but this time without the verbal explanation. This silent *demonstration* requires them to pay close attention to your hand motions throughout each of the steps.

Next, you invite them to **practice** using their nylon cord to tie the knot to an object such as a small tree or a partner's leg while facing the object they are tying the bowline to. This way they learn to tie the knot orientated in the same way as the bowline they will tie to a tree for their shelter set-up.

While everyone is practicing, walk around observing each student's performance to **evaluate** their skill acquisition. Take the time to give specific feedback to each learner and when needed, provide **corrections** for the students who are struggling with this new skill.

At this point you will probably notice that some students are mastering the knot already, so invite them to keep **practicing** but with their eyes closed. While they are taking the new challenge, you can keep monitoring the students who were initially struggling with the skill. If you feel you need more practice time, these students and the rest of the group can now tie a bowline with their eyes closed. Challenge the more proficient learners by asking them to continue **practicing**, but this time with their eyes closed while holding their breath – as if they were underwater in a dark cave and their friend was depending on their ability to quickly tie a bowline.

Step by Step
Skill Oriented Teaching Strategy

Another useful teaching strategy used to instruct skill acquisition is what we call the *"step by step"* strategy. With this strategy the instructor can teach a complex skill to a large group of students in a relatively short period of time.

Imagine having to teach how to put on a climbing harness to a group of 12 students. You can use the *EDP-ECP* teaching strategy, but if there are many steps needed to safely put and adjust a harness, then perhaps a *step by step* form of instruction might be more appropriate.

The *step by step* strategy works well for complex skill instruction because it requires each student to follow the instructor's actions and directions at the same time as the instructor completes the steps to perform the skill. Because a skill such as putting on and adjusting a climbing harness may include many important steps like (1) orienting the harness in the right direction, (2) identifying the inside and outside of the harness, (3) placing your legs in the right leg loops, (4) adjusting and buckling the waist loop, (5) and, if needed, backing up the waist and leg loop buckles.

> The **step by step** strategy works well for complex skill instruction because it requires each student to follow the instructor's actions and directions at the same time as the instructor completes the steps to perform the skill.

The advantage of using this strategy is that everyone will be able to complete the skill at about the same time with no errors. However, this strategy might be less effective in promoting the acquisition and mastery of skills by the students. The *step by step* strategy works well when you need a quick and controlled completion of a skill such as putting a climbing harness on, lifting and adjusting a heavy backpack, dismantling and cleaning a dirty camping stove, and so on. Practice and mastery of these complex skills could come after your initial lesson at a later time.

When using this strategy, remember that it is very important to place your students in a position that will allow them to clearly see you perform each step in the skill you want them to complete. It is also important that each student has the required equipment to complete the skill. Set your expectations in advance and ask that each student waits until the completion of each step before moving to the next one.

As always, make sure that you use clear and precise verbal explanations when demonstrating a step, and assure that everyone is at the same step before introducing the next one. Even with clear and specific explanations and *demonstrations*, do not be surprised if some of your students struggle and take a long time to complete some of the steps. If this happens, quickly help the struggling student or ask a student who has completed the step successfully to assist other learners through *peer teaching*. Remember to be patient in your instruction and to praise student effort and give specific feedback when they have properly completed a step.

Example: Tying a Bowline on a Coil Knot

You plan to teach an emergency tie-in climbing knot known as the "Bowline on a Coil." You get enough climbing rope for everyone to practice and ask them to stand in a circle for your lesson. After giving a rational for the knot and the context in which it can be used, the lesson goes as follows:

1. Ask your students to follow your exact instruction and *demonstration* and to wait when they have successfully completed a step.
2. **Demonstrate** how to measure the length of the rope you will need to complete the knot. *Look around and make sure that everyone has completed this task before moving to the next step.*
3. **Show** students where to place the measured rope on their bellybutton and proceed to wrap the rope in a tight downward spiral at least 3 times around their waist. Remind them that no wrap should cross another. Demonstrate that the running end of the rope should cross their chest, be placed on their shoulder, and then hang there on its own. *Again, look around to make sure that everyone has completed this task before moving to the next step.*
4. **Explain and demonstrate** how the standing end of rope which drops from their bellybutton needs to be looped and placed under the stack of rope around their waist with the standing end against their belly. If done properly, the loop should stay there on its own. *Once everyone has completed this task, move to the next one.*
5. **Show** how to make a bight on the standing end of the rope - which should be running from your loop to the ground. Carefully explain that the bight should enter the loop you have just created. The tip of the bight should stand about 3 inches above the loop. *Wait for everyone to complete this part of the knot before introducing the next step.*
6. Next, **demonstrate** how to take the running end - which has been resting on your shoulder from the beginning - and place its tip through the bight. Indicate that the running end must enter the bight by following the same direction as the rope that has been wrapped around the waist. *Once this*

step has been completed by everyone, introduce the last step. Again, go around the group and help anyone who is struggling with the wrapping of the running end through the bight of the standing rope.

7. Finally, **show** your students how to create a bowline by simultaneously pulling the standing end below the loop and the running end away from each other. Voilà, explain that they now have created a bowline on a coil knot.
8. In order to secure the loose rope section of the running end, **demonstrate and explain** that students should tie a fisherman knot around the whole waist wrap to finish. *Verify that all of your students have properly formed the bowline with the backup and congratulate them for their efforts and ability to follow instructions for a complex skill!*

Whole - Part - Whole
Skill Oriented Teaching Strategy

A popular teaching strategy in Physical Education or sport coaching is known as *"whole-part-whole"*. This teaching strategy takes the instructional principles found in the *EDP-ECP* strategy but adds elements to its sequence by breaking down the skill into distinct motor skill parts.

The instructional sequence begins with the explanation and *demonstration* of the whole skill. Then, if appropriate, it is followed by a practice period similar to the *EDP-ECP* strategy. Once these initial steps are completed, the skill is then broken down into distinct parts so that these distinct parts or "chunks" can be separately practiced, evaluated, corrected, and practiced again until proficiency is achieved. Consequently, the purpose of "chunking" is to improve the mastery of the whole skill by working on its individual and distinct parts. The last phase of this strategy is to link all of these "chunks" into the performance of the whole skill, hence the name of the strategy *"whole-part-whole."* This last step must be offered only to the students who have developed proficiency in all of the skill "chunks." Until each "chunk" of the skill is acquired, a student will be encouraged to practice the distinct parts of the skill.

> The purpose of "chunking" your instruction is to improve the mastery of the whole skill by working on its individual and distinct parts.

This strategy can be very effective when instructing complex motor skills with distinguishable parts such as a cross-country ski double pole push, a Telemark ski turn, or the infamous kayak roll.

Example: Performing a Kayak Roll

Before going to the river for a white-water kayaking class, you rightfully decide to equip your students with an essential kayaking skill – the kayak roll. First make sure that you have enough equipment for each student to practice this new skill and that you have access to a swimming pool or a lake with a beach offering a gradual slope into the water. After giving a rational for the kayak roll and the context in which it can be used; the lesson could go as follows:

First, position your students so that they all can see your *demonstration*. When you have their attention, tell them that soon they will be able to do "this" – as you proceed to perform an effective kayak roll. Once their initial feeling of disbelief has subsided, explain that this skill can be broken down into various parts which can be acquired before completing a full kayak roll.

Note: *Because the possibilities of performing a successful kayak roll during one's first attempt is quite minimal, it would be more appropriate for this skill to move from the demonstration of the whole skill to the breakdown of its chunks instead of asking your students to practice their roll right after your initial demonstration.*

The normal "chunking" for this skill includes (1) becoming accustomed to being underwater in a kayak, (2) performing the hip snap, (3) keeping your head down during the role, (4) placing your paddle blade correctly, and (5) the applying pressure on the blade to initiate the roll.

Therefore, to begin your instruction of the parts of the roll, ask for two volunteers, one of whom could be your co-instructor, to enter the water up to their waists so they can assist you with the first chunk of the roll, which is to be comfortable being under water in a kayak. To help you, the volunteers will each hold one tip of your kayak while you are gently rolling your body under water.

Demonstrate how a person can be relaxed by holding your breath for a long time once you are upside down. When ready, gently tap the bottom hull of your kayak to signal that you are ready to be returned to the surface. Once this *demonstration* has been completed, invite your students to team up and practice this skill.

The rest of the lesson will consist of explaining and demonstrating each "chunk" before allowing students to practice and acquire different parts of the roll.

When some students are ready to put all of the parts of the skill together, you can assist them with their first kayak roll before they attempt to perform a roll on their own without any help.

Physical Manipulation
Skill Oriented Teaching Strategy

When teaching outdoor technical skills, it is possible that you will encounter students who have difficulty learning a new motor skill. Even after a detailed verbal description of the skill and an excellent *demonstration*, some students will still not be able to perform the skill because their orientation or kinetic repertoire of movement is limited or challenged by this new skill. This is when it might be appropriate for you to offer the struggling learner the option to have you assist their movement by performing a *physical manipulation* of their body, limbs, or equipment (i.e., paddle, ski, poles, etc.).

This teaching strategy requires the instructor to physically move, in a slow motion, the learner's body through the proper phases of the motor skill. This will allow the learner to acquire proper kinetic feedback which will lead to a muscular memory of the motion required to perform the motor skill. This strategy can be used until the learner is able to properly perform the skill on their own.

> At times it may be appropriate for you to offer the struggling learner the option to have you assist their movement by performing a **physical manipulation** of their body, limbs, or equipment.

Although *physical manipulation* might be time consuming for the instructor, the personalized, one-on-one instruction nature of this strategy is what will help many students acquire new and complex motor skills. Imagine how beneficial this teaching strategy can be when teaching a paddling stroke, belaying, self-arrest, or the cross-country kick double pole push.

When using this teaching strategy, make sure that the learner is comfortable with you physically touching them before using a *physical manipulation*. Always take the time to ask permission before using this strategy.

Example: Performing a J-stroke

While teaching a canoe stroke lesson you may notice that one of your students is struggling with the J-stroke. You decide to help by offering to provide a *physical manipulation*. The student is comfortable with this option and you proceed by doing the following:

First, ask the learner to come near the shore by the beach so that you can stand in the water beside the canoe.

Take hold of the student's paddle blade with both of your hands and ask the student to relax both arms so that you can move the paddle through the proper phases of the J-stroke.

Begin with the catch phase of the stroke, pausing for a few seconds to emphasize the right placement of the blade and shaft. Then, slowly move the blade in the water through the power phase of the stroke. After a short pause in the middle of this phase, ask the student to pay attention to the change in the angle of the blade when the J-stroke is performed. Pausing at the end of the stroke, let the learner experience the feeling the stroke gives to the upper hand wrist. Finally, move the blade through the recovery phase of the stroke by feathering the blade a few inches over the water.

Repeat this manipulation a few times before asking the learner to attempt the stroke alone.

Prompting Cues
Skill Oriented Teaching Strategy

Another effective strategy for teaching technical skills is using *prompting cues*. *Prompting cues* are verbal, non-verbal, or a combination of both cues used to remind students of key points that they should remember during a specific technical skill.

An effective *prompting cue* uses a single word or a short phrase to create a mental picture of what a student should do to improve performance. For instance, when teaching eddy turns in a paddling class, using the *prompting cue* SAL will quickly remind the students to have a proper speed, angle and lean in order to perform the eddy turn. Of course, this teaching strategy only works if before using this verbal cue you have taken the time to explain and demonstrate what each key element of a good eddy turn implies. But in the end, saying the word "SAL" over the noise of rushing water, beats trying to say, "Don't forget to get enough speed and make sure your angle is about 45° with the eddy line, and most importantly make sure that you both lean your canoe downstream before crossing the eddy." So basically, *prompting cues* are quick easy ways to coach students while they are practicing new skills.

> **Prompting cues** remind students of key points that they should remember during a specific technical skill.

Note that although *prompting cues* are quite useful when teaching motor skills, they can also be used when teaching interpersonal skills such as communication skills and leadership. An example of using prompting cues when instructing communication skills could be to use a non-verbal cue such as pointing to your eyes to remind a student leader to seek eye contact with a group member when talking to them.

To effectively use this strategy, it is also important to explain to your students that you will be using *prompting cues* when observing their skill practice. Doing so will allow your students to prepare themselves to receive verbal and non-verbal cues which will remind them of key elements in their skill performance. You should introduce your *prompting cues* when demonstrating and explaining the various parts of skill. Associating each of these parts with a specific cue, or carefully explaining what you expect them to do when you are cueing, will allow you to use this teaching strategy more effectively.

Example: Basic Rock Climbing Movement

Before letting your students practice their basic rock climbing moves on a small bouldering wall, take the time to explain the principle regarding the placement of a climber's center of gravity over the climber's feet regardless of the angle of the wall. While teaching this, include a verbal prompting cue with this principle since you know that often beginner climbers forget about how to properly load weight on their feet. Your lesson could go as follows:

Position your students so that they all can see your *demonstration*. When you have the attention of all your students, proceed to explain that one of the basic rules in rock climbing is to efficiently use your feet. To do so, explain that a climber's center of gravity should be placed over the climber's feet.

With a good *demonstration* on the bouldering wall, show how placing weight over one's feet allows the foot placement to be more effective. Demonstrate and explain that when you move your hips away from the gently sloping wall, your feet stay well anchored to their footholds.

In contrast, when the wall starts to overhang, demonstrate how your hips must move forward near the wall while your back arches. In this position, your students should notice that your feet are still holding to the wall. At this point you can tell them that when they are practicing, if they hear you say, *"over your feet,"* it will be a reminder to either move their hips closer or farther from the wall so that their feet can carry more weight and be more secure on their footholds.

Next, ask your students to partner up and invite them to practice moving along the bouldering wall, which ideally offers a variety of wall angles. While they are practicing, if you notice that Lia's hips are too close to a gentle slopping section of the bouldering wall, call out: *"Lia – over your feet."* When Lia hears your verbal cue, she can promptly readjust her position by moving her body away from the wall, consequently placing more weight on her feet.

Video Feedback
Skill Oriented Teaching Strategy   LEVEL 2

One of the most effective ways to learn a new physical skill is to see oneself performing the skill in question. Video analysis of athlete performance has been used for decades. The same benefits of seeing one's performance can be provided to students in Outdoor Education mostly because the current audio-video technology makes it possible. Video recording devices are so small and lightweight that they can easily be carried in the field or on a wilderness expedition.

What this teaching strategy can provide to a learner is objective feedback on their performance. As the maxim goes, "a picture is worth one thousand words." Hence using *video feedback* can provide information and understanding that at times even the best verbal feedback cannot accomplish. By seeing oneself, a learner can better appreciate and evaluate body and limb position, movement, angle, and speed throughout the entire skill. Imagine teaching the Telemark ski turn with the help of *video feedback*. After you film a couple of turns, immediately show the learner the video of the performance. This kind of information can be crucial for the student attempting to learn a difficult skill.

The quality in digital videography from devices like tablets, smart phones, and digital cameras with playback screens, has advanced so much that using them for outdoor teaching lessons has proven to be more than adequate. The beauty of these devices is that their digital recording allows you to quickly provide playback, slow-motion replay and keep or discard any recording with the push of a button.

Once again, it would be short-sighted to think that this teaching strategy can only be used for motor skill instruction. It could easily be used for recording and reviewing other skills such as communication, decision making, or feedback.

Example: Hiking Rest Step

While you are leading a small hiking group of students you may find a great section of the trail that is ideal to teach the use of the rest step. Assuming that you have a small computer tablet with you that allows you to capture video images, you chose to use a *video feedback* strategy to help your instruction, since the rest step requires subtle changes in one's regular step.

To use this strategy, you position your students along a steep section of the trail so that they can all see your *demonstration*. When you have their attention, proceed to explain and demonstrate how the rest step is different than a regular hiking step. After presenting the biomechanical elements of the rest step, you can invite each student to practice this new technique by coming up the hill one at the time.

Because you have placed yourself higher on the trail, you can see your students climbing up towards you. Now is when you could take the time to pull out your mini tablet and begin to video record each student while they come up the trail practicing the rest step.

Once each student has reached your position, show a short playback of the hiking technique. Many of them will gain invaluable information about the way they are using the rest step by seeing their own body in motion. After pointing out what they are each doing effectively, praise effort and share areas for improvement. After this feedback session make sure to ask them to practice again.

You can video record the second practice session and this time ask them to self-evaluate their own performance while looking at the video playback. Listening to their commentary will help you assess if they understand the crucial skill elements of the rest step.

Knowledge Oriented Teaching Strategies

Interactive Lecture

Lecture with Seeded Questions

Lecture with Seeded Facts

Lecture with Seeded Q-cards

Leapfrogging

Mystery Challenge

Demonstration

Skill Modeling

Scale Modeling

Guided Discovery

Interactive Lecture
Knowledge Oriented Teaching Strategy

A lot of information can be passed on to students quickly using a traditional lecture strategy, but traditional lectures tend to put students into a passive learning mode without a lot of information retention. Spicing up your lecture in an interactive way while keeping it short and sweet (no more than 10 minutes for younger students and 15 minutes for most adults), can be a really fun way to pass on information.

In an *interactive lecture*, instead of just presenting information, you involve students by asking for their input. You can do this by prompting students with questions or challenging their thinking by asking for their input.

For example, when teaching the history of the Global Positioning System (GPS), instead of just feeding students facts, you can make a timeline with little drawings to serve as clues next to each date. After explaining to students that you are going to explore the history of GPS, ask them to look at the 1960's drawing of a lightbulb next to a satellite. Ask them what was going on in the world during the 1960's? Who launched the first satellite? Etc. Students will share ideas and work together with each other and you to explore the topic.

> In an **interactive lecture**, instead of just presenting information, you involve students by asking for their input. You can do this by prompting students with questions or challenging their thinking by asking for their input.

Another strategy to involve students in an *interactive lecture* is to give each person a card with "YES" on one side and "NO" on the other. As you lecture, ask the class different questions and have everyone hold up a response. You can also wrap up the last couple of minutes by asking questions and having students hold up responses as a form of summative assessment.

Asking students to rate their level of understanding with a thumb up, down, or in between scale also works well when trying to get a grasp on student understanding. This can be done throughout the *interactive lecture* or at the end. So yes, there is still a place for lectures in teaching, just keep it short, sweet, and interactive!

Example: Global Positioning System (GPS) History

For this short lecture on the history of the GPS, prepare a visual aid for the lecture by writing and drawing something similar to the drawing below:

Begin your *interactive lecture* by asking if your students use a GPS device or GPS based app often. Establish with your students that GPS services are commonly used in our modern day lives via our cellular phones, computers, commerce, delivery companies, scientific research, rescue, and government defense department - to name a few.

Then ask if they could tell the story on how the current North American GPS was created. Most likely they will not be able to do so. Consequently, invite them to discover the brief history of the Global Positioning System via an *interactive lecture*.

Explain that the GPS system currently consists of 31 operating satellites in orbit dedicated to the system, but that the system can still work properly with a minimum of 24 satellites. This is called the space segment of the system.

Ask your students if they can help each other decipher the meaning of the images on the GPS history timeline. Start with the first image: **The Light Bulb**. They should come-up with the logical guess that the initial ideal of the GPS system came up in the late 1950's - early 1960's. Ask them if they know what special event happened in 1957 that might have triggered this idea to use space satellites to identify one's position on the surface of the planet. Again, some in the group may suggest that the Soviet Union had launched the first artificial satellite called "Sputnik."

Move along the timeline to the **Dollar Sign**. Again, ask if they can guess what happened in 1973. With a few hints from you they will come up (usually through guessing) that the system was authorized and funded by the US Congress in 1973. Explain that the initial system was named the Defense Navigation Satellite System since the funding was approved for the defense department.

Now ask what happened in 1978? The **Satellite** image will give them a hint. They will guess that the GPS satellites were sent into space. Explain that the first satellite from Block 1 (which included 10 satellites), was launched in 1978 and not completed until 1985.

The next image on the timeline will be a puzzler. The **Exploding KAL007 Airliner** (1983) will most likely not be known by your students, so just tell them the story of the ill-fated Korean civilian airliner (KAL 007), which was shot down by a Soviet interceptor aircraft because the commercial airliner had strayed into prohibited airspace. Explain that the incident was caused by navigational errors. 269 people on board died. Consequently, President Reagan promised that once the GPS system was complete, the US Government would make the positioning system available for civilian use.

The **O.K.** clue on the timeline might once again puzzle your students. Therefore, they might need more prompting from you. If you need to help them, ask this question: "Do you think that building a complex network of 24 satellites can be achieved rapidly?" This should be enough for them to guess that in 1995 the current GPS system was finally completed. If they proposed this answer, praise them again for being so intuitive.

Moving along the timeline, ask your students if they can guess what the **Open Padlock** might mean for the average GPS users. They will guess right away that a system was unlocked. Confirm their assumption and explain that before the year 2000, civilian users such as hunters, anglers, and outdoor recreationists could use handheld GPS (i.e., User Segment) but that the accuracy of the system was limited due to "selective availability." This "error" in the GPS signal was controlled by the Department of Defense to limit the accuracy of the system among non-military users. The Clinton administration discontinued this "selective availability" for safety reasons.

At this point in the *interactive lecture*, ask if anyone has any questions about the development or history of the Global Positioning System created by the US Government.

This *interactive lecture* will normally take you only 10 to 15 minutes to complete, while simultaneously keeping your students fully engaged in the subject.

Lecture with Seeded Questions
Knowledge Oriented Teaching Strategy

Have you ever wanted to spice up a lecture with more student involvement? Have you ever asked a question that nobody seemed able to answer? Have you ever wanted to make a sensitive topic less threatening? If so, then you may want to consider utilizing seeded questions in your next lesson.

Seeded questions are sentences written on a piece of paper that you secretly hand out to students who come early to class. During the class, you make eye contact to cue different students to recite what was written on their piece of paper. These can be profound questions asked just at the right moment, or comments and phrases that fit well into your lecture. Plant a few of these seeds with a handful of students and you suddenly have a class full of people asking questions and sharing comments. This teaching strategy is effective with almost any topic from natural history to hygiene.

When you use *seeded questions*, you create an opportunity for students to step into a new persona for role playing. The group usually livens up and becomes more interested in seeing who is going to say something meaningful next. You could involve anyone - from a shy student to the class clown. However, it is important to carefully select who you choose to give a seeded question card to. Ask only willing volunteers and avoid putting pressure on students who might not feel comfortable at this stage in your course progression. This technique is not meant to dominate the lecture, but only to involve students and ignite *discussion*.

> **Seeded questions** are sentences written on a piece of paper that you secretly hand out to students who come early to class. During the class, you make eye contact to cue different students to recite what was written on their piece of paper.

Traditionally, when teachers instruct using a lecture format, students settle into their seats conditioned to take a passive role. They shut off the interactive valve and expect to be "fed" information in a direct, painless manner. By seeding questions in the audience, students are suddenly forced to become actively involved. They ask pertinent questions (without the pressure of coming up with a good question), which in turn keeps the class on its feet.

This technique tends to be effective when set up well, since students are not only getting the information through an inquisitive channel, but they are also having a really good time. The mystery involved suddenly wakes up the passive learners and gets them to move out of a backseat role and into an active role. In addition to planting questions about the specific topic being taught, throw in a card or two that says something like "hey, this is a really fun class; I can't wait to learn more!" Or, to make sure that everyone is truly listening, try throwing in a card that says something like: "Wow, I really like what you've done with your hair today." This is often said in the context of an extended expedition when everyone's hair looks dramatic and wild. To this question you can respond, "thank you, I'm so glad you noticed that I did my hair up for class today." If anyone is still sitting passively at this point, a goofy question or two definitely wakes them up and gets them laughing.

Example: Hypothermia

When teaching this class, in addition to actually planting questions within the group, you can set a few students up in advance to demonstrate major topics that you want to cover. It's fun to demonstrate the ways a body loses heat by having a few students casually set themselves up in the following positions. Give the first "actor" a card that says "#1 - sit in the snow without a ground pad and shake violently." When you are ready to teach about conduction, make eye contact with the seeded actor and soon she will starts shaking violently while sitting directly on the snow. At first this can throw the class off guard because, if the acting is good, they think it is real. Remain calm and quickly ask the group what is happening.

At this point, the second seeded student asks, "Isn't Lola losing body heat through conduction?"

"Yes, excellent observation," you reply. "Can anyone tell me what 'conduction' is?"

Now the second student continues, "Yes, it is when you lose heat from direct contact between a warm body and a cold one."

"Good observation," you reply. "What can we do to help Lola warm up here?"

At this point, the class engages itself by throwing out ideas on ways to warm Lola up. The big answer to the conduction issue is to put a ground pad between Lola and the snow. The class does this. Once the student is comfortable, go back to the lecture format while re-emphasizing "conduction," and write it on a mylar sheet or white board so that visual learners can recall it easier.

Once this is taken care of, give a cue so that suddenly another student starts shaking from being cold and wet. Go through the same sequence as before, but this time teach about evaporation. When that is done, move on to radiation, respiration, and convection. By the end of the class, if you have a group of 12 students, typically most of them were participants that were given seeded questions ahead of time. It's incredibly rare to work with students who did not absolutely love being involved with seeded questions.

Lecture with Seeded Facts
Knowledge Oriented Teaching Strategy

A *lecture with seeded facts* is similar to a *lecture with seeded questions* in that you subtly hand out little sheets of paper to students before class begins. However, instead of writing questions on the sheets, you write interesting facts related to the lecture that you are about to teach.

There are many ways to pull this off effectively. You can number the facts and then cue the student with the number. You can make a list of who has what fact and then make sure to call on that student when the time comes. Depending on your students and the complexity of the topic, you can even make space for the students to step in on their own when you pause and ask if anyone knows any interesting facts about the topic.

Like *seeded questions*, giving facts to students helps keep those with and without the facts alert and engaged. It can also be incredibly funny to hear different people who are not experts on certain topics spew out wonderful facts in front of their classmates.

This strategy can also be a top choice when you don't know all of the facts yourself. Instead of staring at a notebook or a whiteboard with your prewritten facts, the lecture comes to life as students take the pressure off of you to know everything. They supply the missing information through facts. You can use this strategy with just about any topic from geology to first aid. Students can't get enough of this strategy. There are never dull moments!

Example: Norwegian Spruce Tree

Below are a few facts about Norwegian Spruce trees that can be handed to a few students before a lesson. After starting the lesson, you can ask if anybody knows anything cool about this tree. Soon the students will start sharing the facts that you gave them. Depending on the group and the particular student, some will memorize the facts and recite them as experts, others will inevitably read straight from the card. Either way, it's effective and fun.

Norwegian Spruce Cool Facts

1. Did you know that the tallest measured Norway spruce is 62.26 m (204 feet) tall and grows near Ribnica na Pohorju, Slovenia?

2. A press release from Umea University says that a Norway spruce clone named "Old Tjikko," was carbon dated as 9,550 years old. It is actually the "oldest known living tree."

3. Every Christmas, the Norwegian capital city Oslo provides the cities of London (the Trafalgar square Christmas tree), Edinburgh, and Washington D.C. with a Norway spruce, which is placed in the most central location of each city. This is mainly a sign of gratitude for the aid these countries gave during the Second World War.

Lecture with Seeded Q-cards
Knowledge Oriented Teaching Strategy

In this strategy, you will need to write key words from your lesson on paper or index cards (cue-cards) and distribute them to all of your students before class. Remember, for your lecture to be most effective, it should not be longer than 10 - 15 minutes.

Before starting class, frontload the lesson by telling students that they will need to listen very, very carefully. When the time comes for their "key word" (written on their cue-card), they will yell out their word. If two people yell out a different word at the same time, it creates a perfect moment for the class to work together to come to a consensus on what they think the correct word for the situation should be.

As with the other seeded lecture strategies, the cue-card turns passive learners into active, engaged learners. They become a part of the show instead of the audience. As a teacher, if you feed the expectation for correct key words with energy and excitement, the students will match your energy and force themselves to hold back from exploding with excitement. If done well, you can turn a dull lecture into a lively, entertaining and engaging show!

This strategy involves everyone in the class and requires students to listen very carefully. When the time comes for their "key word" (written on their cue-card), they will yell out their word.

Example: <u>Rock Cycle</u>

Begin this lesson by proudly claiming that you and your students will "Rock this Lecture." Tell them that you will review the basic processes of the rock cycle through a short lecture with audience participation. Distribute the cue-cards randomly, making sure that everyone has a few cue-cards. Explain how they will participate, clarify any possible questions they might have and then proceed with a short lecture, which might look like this:

Instructor: What is the difference between a rock and a mineral? Are rocks made of minerals or do a group of rocks create a mineral?
Lia: I think that minerals are very small, so they are the parts that make rocks.
Instructor: Lia is correct, rocks are made of minerals. For example, granite is composed mainly of quartz and feldspar with minor amounts of mica, amphiboles, and other minerals. But, note that what makes a granite rock is not only the mineral but how the minerals were put together through the geological process.

Instructor: On this planet, and perhaps in the whole solar system, there are only 3 major types of rocks. There are **Igneous Rocks, Sedimentary Rocks** and, uh… I can't remember the last one, cue-card please!
Luc: Metamorphic Rock!
Instructor: Perfect Luc! The three principle types of rocks are **Igneous Rocks, Sedimentary Rocks,** and **Metamorphic Rocks**.

Instructor: Igneous rocks are made through the process of cooling and solidification of magma or lava. Sedimentary rocks are formed by the accumulation or deposition of small particles and subsequent cementation of mineral or organic particles on the floor of… the floor of… cue-card please.
Ajax: The floor of "oceans or other large bodies of water on Earth!"
Instructor: Excellent Ajax! While igneous rocks can be said to have been made through fire, we could say that sedimentary rocks are made through water. While metamorphic rocks are made through…. cue-card please.

Sadie: Pressure! They are made through pressure.
Instructor: Very good Sadie, you are right on.

    The lecture continues with more requests for cue-cards so that all students can be engaged in the lecture. If a student offers the wrong word for a requested cue-card, ask if the word makes sense in this context and invite other students to offer alternative words while guiding them to make the correct choice.

Leapfrogging
Knowledge Oriented Teaching Strategy

Leapfrogging is a perfect teaching strategy to use when traveling through a changing landscape. *Leapfrogging* allows you to teach mini lessons encouraging close student observation through environments that show subtle to dramatic differences. This strategy is especially effective when teaching natural science.

For example, you can begin your lesson at the base of a mountain by introducing the characteristics of a Balsam Fir tree. Students will notice long, flat, and smooth or "friendly" needles. They may observe the height of the tree and the straight nature of the branches. This first observation phase will lay the foundation for the rest of the lesson.

> **Leapfrogging** allows you to teach mini lessons that encourage close student observation through environments that show subtle to dramatic differences. It is a perfect strategy for teaching natural science.

As you hike with your students up the mountain, take time to stop and ask them to observe any changes that they may notice in the Balsam Fir trees. Initially, the changes will be too subtle to be noticeable, but you will be honing observation skills. As you near the top of the mountain, changes in height and needles will become more obvious. Finally, as you head into the exposed upper slopes, the sturdy, stunted Balsam Fir with rounder and shorter needles will look entirely different from its namesake on the lower slopes.

You could use questioning to encourage inquiry and close observation and then introduce the common term "Krumholz", which is the name for different types of stunted trees that grow high up on exposed slopes. Ask students **what** type of tree they think it is. Then ask **why** they think it is so short and crooked looking. **How** did this tree change so much through the different environments?

In addition to teaching plant adaptations, *leapfrogging* is an excellent strategy to use when teaching geology, mountain ecology zones, and river zone changes. It is truly an ideal strategy to use when you can't teach a whole lesson in one place due to a changing environment.

Example: River Estuary

For this lesson, you will paddle canoes down a small river which leads to the ocean (i.e., costal estuary). Before starting your journey, explain to your students that by using a topographic map they will encounter different ecosystems as they travel downstream. Tell them that they will stop their journey at specific location to take UTM coordinates, water data, and biological inventories.

Finally, explain that the goal of the experience is to compare the changes they will observe or measure along their journey to the ocean. Remind them that some of the objectives for their canoe trip are to enjoy their paddling experience, observe the changes in the river environment, and collect scientific information.

Begin your data collection at the canoe put-in. Ask your students to pair up as co-paddlers and co-investigators. Then give them their data collection kits which might include a handheld GPS, a topographic map of the river, a water salinity refractometer, a water digital pH meter, a thermometer, an aquatic triangular net, an aquatic insect identification card, and a note pad to record data. Their data recording sheet could look like this:

Researcher Names				
UTM Coordinates	Water Salinity	Water Temp.	Water pH	Aquatic Insects

At the end of your journey to the sea, after *leapfrogging* along the river and collecting scientific data, ask your students to plot on their maps the location they have collected data. Invite them to compare data between research teams, and to analyze their findings. Ask them if they can answer the following questions:

1. Where does the water reach a salinity above 0.05ppt?
2. Did you find different aquatic insects at the put-in compared to the last data collection location?
3. Does the water temperature go up, down, or remain the same along the river?
4. Does the water pH go up, down, or remain the same along the river?
5. Did you observe changes along the river banks as we were traveling toward the estuary?

Mystery Challenge
Knowledge Oriented Teaching Strategy   LEVEL 4

Teaching through questions is really like facilitating a mystery game. You choose a topic that you want to empower students to explore and then ask them to solve the problem through a series of questions that can only be answered by you with a "Yes" or a "No." Excitement inevitably builds when using this teaching strategy, and questions often take on a competitive urgency as students close in on solving the mystery. *Mystery questions* go great with teachable moments or pre-planned environmental studies topics.

Example: Frost Crack

If you are hiking with students and approach a tree with a long vertical crack in it, stop and put on your "mystery face," ask your students if they can solve the mystery of what happened here, and then let the questions flow. For example:

Student Question: "Is this made from something in nature?"
Answer: "Yes"

Student Question: "Is the crack from an animal?"
Answer: "No"

Student Question: "Did lightning hit this tree?"
Answer: "No"

Student Question: "Are cracks typically on one side of the tree?"
Answer: "Yes"

Student Question: "Did insects do this to the tree?"
Answer: "No"

Student Question: "Is the bark weak here where it split?"
Answer: "Yes" (typically)

Student Question: "Does this have to do with weather?"
Answer: "Yes"

Student Question: "Does this happen in the summer?"
Answer: "No"

Student Question: "Does this happen in the winter?"
Answer: "Yes" (partly - also early spring)

Student Question: "Is it from ice?"
Answer: "Yes"

Student Question: "Does water get into the bark and freeze?"
Answer: "Yes" (the inner bark)

Student Question: "When the water freezes, does it expand?"
Answer: "Yes"

"So, in winter, at the end of the day when the temperature drops quickly or on cold clear days when the tree cools down quickly, sometimes the bark cools quicker than the wood and rips open a long crack in a weak area on the tree. Sometimes it even makes a huge noise like a rifle. The cracks are usually seen in the spring and may even heal during the summer. Cracks that don't heal are often doorways for decay, insects and bacteria."

Demonstration
Knowledge Oriented Teaching Strategy

The *demonstration* teaching strategy goes hand in hand with other strategies. If you are giving a mini-lecture, you can support your lesson by demonstrating the concept you are trying to teach with a model, movement or a prop. Demonstrations give students and opportunity to see, hear, feel and/or experience the concept that they are learning. You will find many examples of *demonstration* throughout this book.

Example: Pack Packing

The *demonstration* strategy works exceptionally well when teaching students how to pack a backpack. It's helpful to lay out all of your clothing, gear, and food items and then **demonstrate** actually putting the items into your backpack while **explaining** to students the principles behind what you are doing.

There are numerous acronyms to help explain the principles, but **ABCDE** tends to cover the basics thoroughly.

- **A** - Accessible (demonstrate items that should be handy)
- **B** - Balanced (demonstrate packing evenly on both sides)
- **C** - Compressed (demonstrate compressing items)
- **D** - Dry (demonstrate ways to keep things dry in the pack)
- **E** - Essential (demonstrate only bringing what you really need)

Be sure to actually **demonstrate** packing instead of just talking about the principles of packing. Students will hold on to the information better if they see the packing in action.

Adding a visual aid to this *demonstration* is also helpful for some learners. A drawing of a backpack that resembles the main compartments is easy for students to follow. We like to picture a pack like a house. You only need your bed at night so put your bedroom on the bottom of your pack with clothes that you don't need during the day. Sometimes you can stuff your shelter around your bedroom since you don't need it handy.

Put your kitchen on top of the bedroom and close to your back because it tends to be heavy with food and pots. Put your "cubby" or "mud room" in the top of your pack because this is the stuff that you want handy by the door to your house. Accessible items include raingear, headlamp, bug net, etc.

As you can see, using a visual aid, an acronym, and a metaphor are helpful in teaching pack packing, but realize that students will not grasp this concept fully unless you actually **demonstrate** packing a pack and them give them an opportunity to apply what they see you demonstrating.

Skill Modeling
Knowledge Oriented Teaching Strategy   LEVEL 7

Sometimes it is impossible to provide students with an authentic experience related to the topic that you are teaching. The location may not be conducive to your topic or it may be unsafe to actually expose your students to a real experience. In these situations, *skill modeling* is a great strategy to use because you can mimic practicing skills in a contrived setting.

For example, when teaching students about the effects of high altitude on their breathing and exhaustion level, it can be hard to simulate a Himalayan mountain in North America. Instead, asking students to do one minute of jumping jacks at your current altitude and then comparing their heart rate and breathing as they try 30 seconds of jumping jacks while breathing only though a straw can be extremely effective. Students immediately feel the difference in oxygen intake and exhaustion even though they may only be at 1,000 feet.

> **Skill modeling** is a great strategy that allows students to mimic practicing skills in a contrived setting when is it unsafe or impractical to perform the actual skill.

There typically aren't too many situations where you have to mimic skill practice in a contrived setting, but when you find yourself in this situation, *skill modeling* is an ideal teaching strategy.

Example: CPR

Skill modeling is a classic strategy to use when teaching CPR. We don't actually do chest compressions on individuals who have a heart rate, but we need to teach students this skill and allow them a chance to practice. The Annie doll was a pioneer in *skill modeling*!

Scale Modeling
Knowledge Oriented Teaching Strategy

A scale model can be used to teach difficult concepts such as geological time. They often represent an accurate physical relationship between the model and the original object (i.e., distance/size) or concept (i.e., time). As a teaching strategy, *scale modeling* allows you to demonstrate properties of an object or concept that are either impossible to actually see and experience, or difficult to incorporate into your lesson.

Scale models help students experience abstract concepts on a human scale. For example, when teaching about the size and distance between planets in the solar system, *scale modeling* a solar walk with various balls sized to scale and distances spread to scale can really help students conceptualize the size relationships and vastness of the solar system.

You can also use *scale modeling* to show geologic changes that happened over vast amounts of time in the mountain range or river valley that you are traveling through. You can show how the land looked millions of years ago compared to what it looks like today using a small model made with dirt, snow, rocks or sand. You could explain the process as it changes or ask students to piece together the mystery by also incorporating the *Mystery Challenge* strategy.

You could ask students to look at the contour lines on a map and build a scale model of what they anticipate the other side of the mountain pass to look like using a scale that corresponds with the contour line intervals. After building their scale, students could draw it and experience the reality of the scale as they hike through the pass the next day.

The size of a grizzly bear compared to the size of a black bear could be created by you or your students with a scale model. In addition, this teaching strategy could be adapted to a historical timeline. For this scenario, you would space your historical events proportionally with time. A climbing rope works great for timelines.

As with most teaching strategies, *scale modeling* opens up a vast array of creative teaching opportunities which can fully engage students in their own learning.

Example: Human – Nature Relationship Through Time

For this lesson, you will need a measuring wheel or a long athletic measuring tape (100m), a topographic map of your teaching location, and a series of bamboo skewers. Before teaching this lesson, you will also need to print and laminate a series of dates with corresponding distances in feet or meters.

The lesson will involve a short walk outdoors of about 1.5 miles or 2.4 kilometers. Try to use a strait trail along a river or a large field. The ideal trail is a path that allows you to see the beginning and the end of your short walk. The length of the walk (one way) should have a distance of 4000 feet / 0.75 mile or 1220 m / 1.2 km.

When you meet your students explain that you would like to take a little walk with them through time. Explain that this walk will allow them to evaluate and appreciate the long relationship between "Humans" and "Nature." Mention that during your journey each of them will be invited share facts about the significant events along the Human-Nature journey. Finally, explain that in this *scale modeling* exercise, 1 foot will correspond to 100 years (i.e., 1 meter = 327 years).

At the begging of the hike, ask for a volunteer to be in charge of measuring using the measuring wheel or tape. Distribute bamboo skewers (i.e., mini-post sign) with their laminated dates and distances to the rest of the students. Tell them that they will be in charge of planning their mini-post sign at the appropriate distance along the journey as well as preparing a short presentation about the significant Human-Nature relationship associated with this time period. By the end of your time travel hike, you will have set-up 13 stations.

This *scale modeling* activity works best if you lay the course first and then do the instruction on your walk back. Below is the list of significant events along the Human-Nature Relationship journey:

Stations	Distance	Year	Event
1	0	Today	Anthropocene Era with industrial farming and a counter movement toward organic and local food production/consumption.
2	1 foot 5 inches	1901	First commercially successful combustion engine farm tractor is introduced in England.

3	1 foot 5 inches	1868	Steam powered tractors are introduced in modern agriculture.
4	60 feet	6000 years ago	First use of light wooden ploughs in Mesopotamia (i.e., Modern day Iraq).
5	85 feet	8500 years ago	Evidence of cattle domestication in Turkey.
7	90 feet	9000 years ago	Domestication of cattle and chickens in Mehrgarh (i.e., Modern day Pakistan).
8	105 feet	10,500 years ago	Neolithic Revolution with the first agricultural revolution begins in the ancient Fertile Crescent (i.e., The Fertile Crescent is a crescent-shaped region in the Middle East, spanning modern-day Iraq, Israel, Palestinian Territories, Syria, Lebanon, Egypt, and Jordan).
9	400 feet	40,000 years ago	**Homo Sapiens** (300,000 years ago to present) Homo Sapiens (i.e., modern man) are the sole bipedal humanoids. The have spread all over the surface of the planet and even across the Bering Strait to North America.
10	4000 feet (0.75 miles)	400,000 years ago	**Homo Neanderthalensis** (400,000 and 40,000 years ago) Neanderthals were the first early humans to wear necessary clothing since they lived in glacial environments. They may have been the first early human species to have language, bury their dead, and exhibit symbolic behavior.
	From this location, use the topo graphic map to tell the rest of the Human-Nature Relationship.		
11	3.4 miles	1.89 million years ago	**Homo Erectus** (1.89 mya and 143,000 years ago) There is evidence that individuals of Homo Erectus were the first early humans to make hearths, to eat significant amount of animal meat and bone marrow, and to care for the old and weak. It was the longest-lived species on our family tree, surviving more than nine times as long as our own species.
12	4.5 miles	2.4 million years ago	**Homo Habilis** (2.4 and 1.4 mya) Its name, which means 'handy man', was given because when it was discovered at Olduvai Gorge in the early 1960s, this species was thought to represent the first stone toolmaker.
13	6 miles	3.85 million years ago	**Australopithecus Afarensis** (3.85 and 2.95 mya). This species, to which the 'Lucy' skeleton belongs, has apelike proportions of the face and braincase and strong arms with curved fingers adapted to climbing trees, but small canine teeth and a body that stood and walked upright on arched feet.

By adding images to each of these stations representing the main topic, the peer to peer instruction will be more interesting for everyone.

Finally, at the end of each student quick presentation, ask these two simple questions: "How did these humanoids manage to feed themselves?" and "How connected were they with the land?"

Soon your students will notice that for a large majority of our existence on this planet, we (i.e., humanoids) have lived closely with the land. We have mostly survived as hunters and gatherers. Farming, and especially modern agriculture, is a very recent development for our species.

End the journey back to the present time by reading this paragraph inspired by Harrison Brown:

> "In Harrison Brown's classic book, *The Challenge of Man's Future* (1954), there is the interesting hypothesis that our species is so close to the earth we cannot forget physiologically or psychologically our long inheritance. Since the earth is approximatively 4.5 billion years old, if we reduce this time span to 365 days, our species "Homo Sapiens" with his recent emergence, about 300 thousand years ago, has been on the earth only 34.5 minutes. It has been only 10 thousand years since our species had its Neolithic Revolution—a mere 1.2 minute of the time span of our planet's existence. And it's been less than a second out of this clock since we changed from a purely hunting, fishing, and agrarian sort of life about a hundred years ago—less than a second from a life regulated by the seasons, by primitive conditions, adjusting oneself to the vagaries of climate and challenge that life then involved, less than a second out of our human history."

Guided Discovery
Knowledge Oriented Teaching Strategy

Outdoor Education scholar, Donald Hammerman, often said, "Telling is not Teaching." For good measure, Dr. Hammerman was a fervent proponent of using a teaching strategy that engages students in the learning process whenever appropriate. He called it the "exploratory learning" approach to teaching. Using an *exploratory learning* strategy means that the role of the teacher is not to tell the facts, concepts or values that need to be learned, but simply to facilitate learners in exploring and discovering the answers to what they are studying or observing.

> **"Telling is not Teaching."**
> -Donald Hammerman

Through careful questioning, you can help learners find answers to their own observations about the natural world, human behaviors, or even technical problems. To use this strategy, it is helpful if an instructor knows the answers to the mystery at hand, but it is not always critical. What is important is that the student will develop curiosity and a desire to learn. For this strategy to work, you must carefully listen to the students' answers so that your next question can build upon what the students have discovered so far. Ultimately, patience and good open-ended questioning will allow the learners to find the final answer through their own observations and reflections.

An *exploratory learning* strategy can be applied to various instructional situations. Consider the following teaching sample:

Example: Pocket Gopher Castings

On early spring courses, one natural history treasure that covers the Rocky Mountains are the infamous pocket gopher castings that appear once the snow melts. These "snakelike" dirt formations which run all over the mountain meadows are perfect natural wonders for the *exploratory learning* strategy. Try to hold back your urge to tell students what these strange formations are. Instead, let them discover for themselves the story behind these mysterious dirt veins. When you find a fresh collection of castings or eskers, try asking a series of questions that will help students learn about what they are observing. If you use this teaching strategy, your conversation with your students could look like this:

Instructor: "Have you noticed all of these strange snakelike dirt formations on the ground? I wonder what they are."
Students: "Yeah, these are strange, they look like someone laid dirt over the ground, what are they?"

Instructor: "Well, let's see what we can learn by observing them more carefully" (Remember that you know what they are, you just don't want to tell your students without getting them more involved in the learning process.)

Instructor: "Let's break one apart to see if they are made of solid dirt or if they are hollow."
Students: "They are solid pieces of dirt."

Instructor: "Do they seem to have a pattern or are they built randomly?" (Notice here that you just inserted a hint regarding the origin of these formations).
Students: "They appear to be random."

Instructor: "Do they have a starting point?"
Students: "Well, it seems that this one starts here and then branches out in various directions."

Instructor: "Let's look at the starting point that you found and see what we can learn from it."
Students: "Look, there's a hole in the ground, like a small tunnel."

Instructor: "A tunnel, interesting, do you think that the underground tunnel and the dirt formations on the surface are related?"
Students: "Yes, maybe the dirt on the surface came from the tunnel."

Instructor: "This makes sense, so what or who do you think moved the dirt from the tunnel to the surface?"
Students: "Some kind of underground living animal such as a mole."

Instructor: "Right, some insectivores like moles or small rodents like the pocket gopher live in subterranean tunnels. But why would these small mammals come on the surface to place material from their excavation?"

Students: "Maybe it is because they have no other place to move it."
Instructor: "That would make sense, but why would they place that material in compacted and continuous dirt formations? Why don't they randomly distribute the excavation material on the surface?"

At this point, the faces of your students might show perplexity and struggle. It is time for you to give them a hint, so try following up with this observation.

Instructor: "The more I look at these formations, the more they remind me of negative copies of subterranean tunnels, like a casting of a tunnel. What do you think?"
Students: "Right, they do look like tunnels, but more like a bronze casting. Is it possible that the little animal placed the excavation material in tunnels?"

Instructor: "Yes, it's quite possible, but where is the tunnel?"
Students: "I know, it melted away, it was a snow tunnel."

Instructor: "Exactly, elementary my dear Watson. These casting are commonly found in spring just after the snow melts, later on they will disappear during the summer months."

At this point, ask a volunteer to explain the story behind these dirt castings. It will often sound like this:

Student: "In the winter, these small subterranean animals cannot dig their tunnels as usual by pushing the dirt aside because the earth is hard, so they dig to the surface that is now covered with snow and dig snow tunnels that they will later use to discard the dirt from their subterranean excavations. When the snow melts in spring, the remaining dirt castings are found on the surface."

Instructor: "Very good, you have resolved this mystery. Now, let me tell you that a pocket gopher is probably responsible for this amazing engineering feat."

If you feel that the students are curious and intrigued by this little animal and its ingenious behavior, you should certainly tell them more about pocket gophers.

Value Oriented Teaching Strategies

Quotes and Readings

Personal Journaling

Group Journaling

Visual (Guided) Imagery

Case Study

Nature Awareness Activities

Quotes and Readings
Value Oriented Teaching Strategy

"Life is either a daring adventure, or nothing!"

–Helen Keller

Beginning or ending the day with a quote or short reading inevitably frames that day as being special. As a value-oriented teaching strategy, quotes have the power to teach us more in a minute or two than any other strategy. They are especially good at sparking deep thinking and reflection in students as they hike, paddle, or participate in other activities. Revisiting the quote multiple times throughout the day or at the end of the day or course can also spark a meaningful *discussion*.

This teaching strategy can passively or actively engage students. You can read or recite quotes to your students, or you can provide each student with a pile of quotes to keep with their personal journal at the beginning of the course. At an evening meeting it can be powerful to ask students to share a quote that speaks to them while also explaining what they find meaningful in it. This turns the sharing time over to them and becomes not only engaging, but also quite memorable. Never underestimate the power of the right quote at the right time. Quotes can be life changing.

Example: Quote
After a long day, you could close your evening gathering with the following quotes:

"We are all better than we know;
If only we can be brought to realize this,
We may never again be prepared
To settle for anything else."
-Kurt Hahn

"I dwell in possibility."
-Emily Dickinson

In addition to using quotes, readings can be extremely effective in summarizing or teaching lessons after a group experiences a common event together. Maybe it has been a difficult day of hiking and everyone is about to go to bed tired, making little progress with a lot of effort. Pulling the group together for a 15-minute reading that highlights Alexander Mackenzie's 1793 overland crossing of Canada to the Pacific Ocean, or Lewis and Clark's similar struggles moving through the mountains in 1805, offers a powerful lesson in pushing forward amidst adversity. Using *quotes and readings* to process any type of learning experience with your students often sets them up for tackling challenges ahead.

When *quotes and readings* don't fit, try using a special word as teaching tool. Words can be used as reminders or reflections. Perhaps at the end of the day your group is sitting and watching an amazing sunset. No one says anything for a very long time, and then you share a special word to encourage reflection.

Example: Special Word

During a reflective moment, try sharing this Inuit word:

"Koviashuvik,"

"Total awareness of present moment and place with quiet joy and without desire."

Often you need not say anything more.

Another way to use single words is to think of them as "power words." Try giving students a list of some potential power words at the start of your course or sharing your power word and empowering students to think of words that inspire and help them. Power words are meant to be repeated often so that when you are struggling with something, they are easy for your brain to retrieve and return to your consciousness automatically. They can be especially helpful when students start to give up or lose confidence in their abilities.

Example: Power Word

"Unstoppable"

Personal Journaling
Value Oriented Teaching Strategy

Journal writing dates back to the days of the Roman Empire. Through history, some wrote of journeys, others of inward emotions, and yet even more recorded personal reflections of historical events. As a teaching strategy, *personal journaling* is a perfect tool for encouraging the recording of events, self-reflection, scientific observation, information documentation, and funny things that people say.

There are many benefits to keeping personal journals. Encouraging students to record and document events is a teaching strategy for reflection and exploration of ideas of interest to the student. As students document the course of the day or reflections from the front-country, they pull out pieces that are personally meaningful to them and write them down. This type of recap inevitably leads the writer to self-reflection.

Some students are very good at reflecting on their own, while others may find it more difficult. For students who struggle with self-reflection through writing, framing some journal activities with tools and guidance can be helpful.

> **Personal journaling** can be a powerful teaching strategy for reflection and exploration of ideas of interest to the student.

Encouraging students to reflect on their own feelings can ultimately strengthen their intrapersonal skills while indirectly helping them come to know themselves better. When students are homesick, encouraging them to write a letter in their personal journal to someone back home typically helps ease the pain of separation.

Personal journals also provide an excellent tool for enhancing observation skills. Before students record scientific observations in their journals, they must look closely and study the outside world around them. They may need to look at subtle details in nature to determine if they saw a Tufted Titmouse or a Nuthatch. Then they may want to refer to a bird field guide to see if they are accurate. A student may go on to draw this bird in a personal journal and write a description below the drawing with the date and location of where the bird was spotted. Throughout this process, your student is not only engaged and focused, but also completely immersed in the wonders of nature.

In addition, you can encourage students to create a section in their journals for class notes. Here they can document information learned from the lessons taught while they are in the field and any indirect information that they have learned that is of value to them. The journal inevitably becomes a resource to refer to for valuable information.

Journal writing is typically not graded on expeditions, environmental programs or summer camp trips, and in many instances is not read by anyone other than the student. In other instances, journals can be used for formative assessment or to establish an ongoing written dialog between the student and the instructor.

You can also hand out small personal journals for students on courses with specific goals targeting improved self-esteem. Supplying each person with their own journal kit that includes a vast supply of positive, inspirational *quotes* along with structured downtime for journaling can be an invaluable strategy for encouraging reflection and personal growth.

> **Personal Journal Ideas**
>
> Personal observations, reflections or reference sections
>
> Letters to current self, future self, family, or friends
>
> Class notes, environmental notes
>
> Schedules & activities
>
> Nature drawings
>
> Funny drawings or cartoons or habits
>
> Funny nicknames

When a course is over, or the years go by, a written journal can be an incredibly rewarding book to revisit. Journals hold memories that otherwise would be lost. They are treasure chests of poems, songs, sketches, notes, *quotes*, reflections, jokes, and more. Sometimes revisiting an old journal allows students an opportunity to go back in time to re-learn lessons or rediscover insights about themselves all over again. What a powerful teaching tool!

Group Journaling
Value Oriented Teaching Strategy

When framed effectively and driven by motivated instructors and students, group journals inevitably unite people. As a teaching strategy, group journals are a tool for documenting events, recording class information, and creating a forum for sharing stories, poems, drawings, quotes, jokes, readings, and more within a group. Group journals reflect the pulse of the course. They can be fun and entertaining, or simply direct and factual. Interpersonal skills can be strengthened as students learn more ways to celebrate and interact with each other.

Framing the integration of a group journal is an art. You will have more likelihood of truly engaging the group through *group journaling* if you first create a fun and inviting bound journal booklet that you and the students can be proud of. Just handing the group a blank notebook doesn't typically go very far. But, if you spend a few hours creating a journal accessory kit that includes color pencils, scissors, glue stick, magazine photos of wilderness areas, relevant cartoons, and famous quotes, you are off to a great start. Also, attaching a pen to the journal using duct tape and a nylon cord will ensure that there is always a writing utensil on hand.

Ideas for a Group Journal Material Kit

Pencil sharpener, colored pencils & pen

Glue stick or tape

Collection of meaningful quotes, special words & "power words"

Magazine pictures of the outdoors

Maps

Small bag for materials

A bag for weatherproofing

Before handing the journal over, attaching magazine photos, adding quotes, and documenting course expectations that the group brainstormed can help set the students up for success. When using a group journal strategy, including a small map of the area you will be traveling through as well as a sign-up sheet for journal leaders will also go a long way in moving this teaching tool forward.

As the course progresses, encourage students to write, draw, or document events as they see them. Before you start a class, ask who is documenting it in the group journal today. When someone says something memorable, ask who is writing down that quote in the group journal. On mornings before moving, ask who is signed up to be the journal leader for the day. Pass the journal to the leader to carry and keep dry. That is now part of their responsibility. Before you know it, if you frame it well, you will not need to ask students about the group journal, it will become a part of the family with its accessory kit tagging along and spurring creativity.

Group Journal Content Ideas

- Course objectives
- Course expectations
- Course themes
- Map of the route
- Calendar of the course
- Class notes
- Nature nuggets
- List of bird, plants and animals seen on the course
- Daily leader log & leadership tasks
- Song list
- Recommended booklist
- Student quotes of the day
- Poems or stories written by students
- Published quotes and short stories read to the group
- Student reflections
- Drawings & cartoons

At the end of a course, depending on the age of your students and the type of program that you are leading, you may want to have everyone write down contact information. Technology makes sharing documents and photos effortless these days, so you can scan and send everyone an electronic color copy of this priceless book of memories or print copies of it in town. Just like the personal journal, days or even years later, students will be able to revisit their group journal, taking a trip back in time to ignite fun memories, relearn lessons, and rediscover valuable insights that they gleaned from each other in days past.

Example: <u>Student Reflection:</u>
"I like the feeling of crossing over into a new world. Everything works like clockwork. All of nature is in harmony. There's no need for anything else. It makes you feel alive because you're a part of the food chain (in Alaska)." - Ross

Example: <u>Student Funny Quotes:</u>
"I weigh as much as a female caribou." - Jeremy
"How cool would it be if your sweat was an insect repellent?" - Matt
"In about three minutes I'm going to start thinking about thinking about hiking." - Ryan
"Wait you guys...I'm trailing off the end of the group here. I'm like the injured gazelle of the herd, the one that's bait for the lions." - Dara

Example: <u>Group Journal Student Song:</u>
I SMELL BAD
By Alice, Stephanie, Erin, Sriatha, and Jeremy
(Sung to the tune of James Brown's "I feel good.")

I smell bad; I knew that I would now,
I smell bad; I knew that I would now,
    So bad, so bad, I smell you....
I smell ripe; I hope that's alright,
I smell ripe, I hope that's alright.
    So ripe, so ripe, I smell you...
When I'm sleeping in my tent,
I wonder where my deodorant went
And when I smell my sleeping bag,
You know it makes me want to gag.

I smell reek, haven't showered for a week.
I smell reek, from my head to my feet.
    So reek, so reek, I smell you!

Visual (Guided) Imagery
Value Oriented Teaching Strategy   LEVEL 1

Visual imagery begins as thoughts flow through the brain. Even though nothing is actually happening, the brain may perceive smells, tastes, sounds, images, and physical touch. *Visual imagery* is a powerful strategy that has the potential to be applied to multiple teaching situations. It can be used to hook students on a topic, inform students about elements of a specific lesson, or help students mentally practice physical skills.

Imagine teaching the rock cycle by talking students through the journey of igneous, metamorphic, and sedimentary rocks. You could use this to "hook" your students on the topic or to extend a hands-on lesson.

> When **visual imagery** is used as a teaching strategy, students can be transported to the center of the Earth, sent back in time, or placed on a difficult rock climbing route to rehearse moves.

When *visual imagery* is used as a teaching strategy, students can be transported to the center of the Earth, sent back in time, or placed on a difficult rock climbing route that they rehearse and "practice" moving through while invoking strategies and emotions.

You can ask your students to relax, close their eyes, and listen to a narration. This narration may describe an environment, a context, or a behavior in specific detail. Students are often at the center of the imagery, sometimes picturing themselves in a very different place. After walking through the visualization, pause for silent time. The absence of noise makes room for self-reflection that can set your students up for genuine growth.

Example: Cave Formation

After exploring for a while in an underground cave, ask your students to turn off their lights and lay quietly in total darkness. First, simply give students an opportunity to relax and listen while experiencing the pace and peace of nature. After some time, begin guiding students on a *visual imagery* journey.

"Imagine that you are a shell creature, swimming in a vast sea millions of years ago. After you die, picture your shell sinking down to the floor of the lake and remaining there. Imagine time going by slowly...year after year... for many, many years.

Picture other creatures dying and falling on top of you, piling up and building layers upon layers upon more layers of shells on top of you over millions of years. As time passes, you feel more and more pressure from the weight above. You feel yourself getting squished so hard that over time, you and all of the other shell deposits form into limestone rock. Your shell is just one tiny piece of a massive layer of limestone. It's dark down here.

One day some water starts to drip by you. Soon more water drips... and then more. You see some other shell creatures wash away. This erosion doesn't happen quickly, but takes many, many years.

As time continues to tick on, you notice that the water starts to carve out a passageway. It's small at first, but over time, it grows and grows and grows. As it gets bigger, you notice the water carving out long, long sections underground.

> History teaches powerful lessons when framed in a way that we can grow from.

Eventually, you don't feel much water anymore. Instead you feel a breeze. You think there is a small opening somewhere letting the breeze flow through. It continues over many years.

At this point, you can elaborate more on the details of cave formation and then bring the imagery back to the present.

One day you notice lights and voices and images below you. People seem to have come to this place you call home. They turn off their lights and lay down quietly... thinking about your journey over time."

Case Study
Value Oriented Teaching Strategy

Using a *case study* teaching strategy allows students to become familiar with a real-life event that occurred in the past. After listening to a summary of the actual event, students are challenged to come up with solutions to avoid the catastrophe, correct an escalating error, or respond in a manner that could alter the outcome of the event.

History teaches powerful lessons when framed in a way that we can grow from. Allowing students to put on the lens of the decision makers in an actual scenario empowers them to think through the decision-making process. It is a perfect strategy to use when teaching decision making or how to manage risks related to subjective or objective hazards. It can also set students up to analyze the consequences of a hazard vs. the likelihood of a hazard by breaking apart the steps taken in a particular historical case.

Case studies can empower students to look at how groups communicate and resolve conflicts with each other and how this process can influence the outcome of a situation.

Example: <u>Evacuation Dilemma</u>

This *case study* could be used with a group of college students studying Adventure Education. The *case study* could be introduced during an outdoor expedition that focuses mainly on leadership and decision-making skills. Create small groups of two or three students to review, analyze, and find solutions to the *case study*. Distribute copies of the *case study* and give the groups plenty of time to complete the exercise. Be ready to assist the groups to clarify the *case study* or the assignment.

Title: Evacuation Dilemma

Location: Remote established campsite in the White Mountain National Forest, New Hampshire

Group: 10 students and 2 instructors. Most students have a good fitness level but very little hiking experience.

Day & Time: Saturday, October 26th. The 7th day of an 8-day hiking trip. It is 4:00pm.

Scenario: The first hiking group (i.e., 5 students and 1 instructor) arrives at the established campsite. They review the days' experience and set-up camp while waiting for the rest of the class to arrive.

At 4:20pm a middle-aged male solo hiker arrives at the campsite and asks if he could share the same site for the night. The group leader explains that another group of 5 will soon join them but that the solo hikers is most welcome to stay if he does not mind sharing the site with 12 other campers. The man acknowledges the situation and accepts the invitation to stay for the night.

Around 5:15pm, the remaining members of the group have still not arrived at the designated campsite. The instructor tells the students to begin preparing dinner. As the instructor is getting ready to contact her co-instructor using a two-way radio, she notices that the solo hiker is walking with a limp and seems to be moving around the site with a confused look on his face.

When the leader approaches the man, she notices that the right side of his body is stiff and that the right side of his face is sagging. When talking with him, it is obvious that his speech is laborious.

After completing a quick patient assessment, the group leader suspects the middle age man is experiencing a potential stroke. His medical history indicates that he normally carries anticoagulants (i.e., blood thinner) medication. The instructor helps the man look for his medication, but they cannot find it.

The instructor has a first aid kit with her and some over the counter medication such as aspirin, but she does not have the inReach device which could be used to initiate an evacuation. Her co-leader with the other group has the inReach device.

The instructor at the campsite knows that the trailhead is only 3 miles away on an easy flat trail. But she wonders now what to do since she cannot reach her co-instructor who has the inReach device. She knows that a helicopter rescue is possible from this campsite, but she also knows that the pilots do not like to fly rescues at night, and it is already 5:30pm.

She knows that the solo hiker can move on his own but that his walking abilities are affected by the potential stroke. She knows that she has enough students with her to send a runner party to seek help but wonders where to send them. Should they go towards the trailhead, where there is a ranger station with a public phone, or towards the other hiking group which has the inReach device? All she knows is that the medical condition of the solo hiker is serious and that he needs to be brought to a hospital as soon as possible.

Questions:

What should the instructor prioritize in her decision making?

What are all of the options that she has in this situation?

What would you do if you were in this situation?

What would be your plan of action? What back-up plan would you also include in your plan?

What could have happened in the expedition planning stage to help prevent this type of dilemma?

Nature Awareness Activities
Value Oriented Teaching Strategy

Using *nature awareness activities* as a teaching strategy is especially powerful due to the emotional response that these activities can trigger. These activities can help students connect with nature on a physical and emotional level, create a contemplative mood, tune students into the beauty of nature, or reveal insights into the way nature works. Of course, using the nature awareness teaching strategy can also simply empower students to have fun while being immersed in the natural environment.

Joseph Cornell was a pioneer in creating activities that enable students to isolate their senses in order to discover nature in a special way. When student senses are engaged and curiosity is tapped, the stage is set for their innate sense of wonder to come alive. As you immerse students in *nature awareness activities*, learning occurs as students engage their sense of wonder through sensory immersion as they see, feel, smell, hear, or taste!

It's important to acknowledge that taking students hiking or backpacking is not the same as intentionally framing and using a nature awareness activity. The difference is the intentionality and the lens. Frontloading is essential along with meaningful reflection.

Example: Micro-Hike

Set up this classic nature awareness activity by asking your students to find an interesting section in the terrain that they are in and marking out a four to five-foot section. Ask everyone to get down on their stomachs at one end of the "trail." Their "hiking" journey will take them very slowly, inch by inch over the terrain.

As they crawl, students should focus in on the micro-world beneath them. If you have access to magnifying glasses, give one to each student and ask them all to pretend that they are seeing the world through the eyes of an ant. They should try to keep their eyes no higher than one foot off the ground. In no time they will start noticing spiders, broken sticks, pinecone parts and more.

To aid in the discovery and help ignite imaginations, you can ask your students some questions. Joseph Cornell came up with the following that may help get you started or thinking about the micro environment that you are in:

- What kind of world are you traveling through right now?
- Who are your nearest neighbors?
- Are they friendly?
- Do they work hard?
- What is that spider going to do - eat you or take you for a ride?
- What would it be like to be that metallic green beetle? How does he spend his day?

After going on the micro-hike, bring the group together and have them share what they found. This can be done with partners or through small group sharing at first, and then the main highlights could be shared with the entire group. You can also skip the partners and go straight to a whole group reflection.

Multi Oriented Teaching Strategies

Art

Music

Storytelling

Student Storytelling

Puppetry

Student Puppetry

Role-Play

Theatrics

Skits

Role Modeling

Discussion

Debate

Exploratory Learning

Socratic Method

Games

Problem Solving

Simulation

Solo Experience

Peer Teaching

Service Learning

Art
Multi Oriented Teaching Strategy

Using *art* as a teaching strategy is often misunderstood. There are hundreds of ways to incorporate *art*, but it can easily get overlooked especially when working with older students. Remember, you don't have to be an "artist" to use art as a teaching strategy. You just have to have a vision. Your students don't have to be artists either, just growth-minded learners.

Art, for example, can be used as a fundamental tool for teaching map reading in multiple ways. You can have students build a three-dimensional sand or snow mountain that represents a two-dimensional mountain on a topographic map. You can have them draw the contour lines with their fingers or string. Take this lesson to the next level by having small groups draw a map of other group's mountains to see how accurately they can transfer a three-dimensional object onto a two-dimensional piece of paper. After all, when you travel through the mountains, that's what you do on a constant basis. Focusing on maps through art will inevitably help students understand map reading on a deeper level and refine navigational skills.

Another way to help students visualize the landscape from the map is to have them draw the other side of a pass that you will be traveling over the next day. Students should look closely at a topographic map to determine what the landscape looks like on the other side, and then either build the landscape in sand or draw it on a piece of paper. The more practice students get looking closely at maps and visualizing the landscape, the better map-readers they will become. After crossing the pass, they can compare their drawing to the view at hand.

Art is also effective in helping visual learners comprehend concepts. If you verbally explain how lightning is formed, some students may understand. If you draw a picture of a cloud over the land that illustrates the positive charges and the negative charges present, you will clarify your topic visually, thus helping more students grasp the concept. You could even take it to another level by drawing a cloud and land in the dirt and having students stand in the cloud and on the land and act as protons and neutrons moving around during a thunderstorm to see how they create lightning.

After demonstrating bear hang systems and having your students practice different hang techniques, ask them to draw and label each system that they built in their notebook. You could also ask them to draw knots after they learn how to tie them.

Art can also be used to encourage creativity and personal sharing among your students. Giving students a personal or group journal with colored pencils and providing time and space for them to express themselves often goes a long way. In addition, students can take colorful class notes to help remember lessons. You'll find more details on this in the *group journaling* section.

Since learning engages the physiology, students typically comprehend more effectively when they use their senses and their bodies. In this strategy, *art* is used as a tool for aiding comprehension and helping with reflection to deepen understanding. Drawings are not meant to be masterpieces (although some are), but really representations and fun scribbles. Incorporating *art* as a teaching strategy can therefore enhance learning substantially.

Example: Animal Adaptation

After teaching a lesson on how animals adapt to the environment that you are traveling through, give students an opportunity to create the "perfectly adapted animal." Find a durable area and have your students collect natural materials to build their animal. Pinecones, dirt, rocks, branches, and bark work well. If building isn't an option, ask students to draw their animal. After the masterpieces are completed, have the group travel around the area and hear from each artist/naturalist details about their animal and how it is adapted to this environment.

Music
Multi Oriented Teaching Strategy

Music is fun! It is a common thread woven throughout humanity that can typically pull a group together faster than just about anything. Using *music* as a teaching strategy can be truly rewarding and memorable for your students.

There are many ways to incorporate *music* into your teaching. It works well with lessons that incorporate multiple teaching strategies. You can introduce a lesson with a musical "hook", teach some basic content, and then hand off the information to student groups with the request that they create a song about the topic they were given. This serves to reinforce the content while fully engaging your students.

Music can also be used to teach leadership and perseverance. It is an incredibly effective tool in harsh conditions. When your group is making breakfast in snow kitchens in 35 degree sleet for days on end, nothing is more powerful than an upbeat instructor team that walks around each morning serenading cold, wet students. *Music* is sunshine amidst the icy rain. Inevitably, students will begin singing loudly and drumming on whatever happens to be around. Before you know it, they will start singing on their own and serenading others to keep spirits up.

Music works well with lessons that incorporate multiple teaching strategies. It is also a powerful strategy for building rapport with your group.

You can also carry instruments into the backcountry or use them in basecamps. We've carried penny whistles, recorders, harmonicas and ukuleles, and have been in the backcountry with co-instructors who carried small or full-size guitars on month-long courses. Walking around camp and gently waking students up with a ukulele creates a beautiful tone. Students love it! They also love listening to and singing songs played after dinner or at an evening meeting while hanging out together. *Music* is a powerful strategy for building rapport with your students.

A ukulele is a perfect instrument for building rapport because it is so easy to learn. A few students typically want to try playing it in the field and love one-on-one lesson time with an instructor. Since students can go home after a course and buy a decent one for about $50, we've seen *music* with a ukulele turn into a major rapport-building highlight, especially with inner city kids.

Songs are also a great tool for distracting exhausted students while they hike or paddle. *Games* with songs, traveling songs, or just about any form of song can work wonders as a strategy for teaching students that they have more in them than they know.

After a hard day, it is important to join together with your students and reflect upon the things that they learned from the day. If *music* was used, it will no doubt emerge as a highlight that helped keep spirits going.

Example: Nocturnal Animal Rap

After introducing a natural history topic such as nocturnal animals, and teaching some basic information about bats, raccoons, opossums, and coyotes, try integrating *music*. Break your students up into small groups and have each team come up with a "Rap" that explains and praises their particular animal. Give groups ten minutes together to brainstorm their song, and you will be amazed at what your students will come up with. After creating their "Raps," have the student groups present their songs to each other. The "Raps" will not only reinforce the information that you want your students to know, but it will also demonstrate a fun way to pass on information while also building community!

Storytelling
Multi Oriented Teaching Strategy

Stories are the soul of learning and teaching. As one of the oldest forms of communication common to all humanity, stories are the historical remains or imaginings of things that have come or will come. Stories help us make meaning out of events or content and therefore truly permeate all aspects of learning. As a teaching strategy, *storytelling* can be incredibly powerful because emotion is evoked while cognitive information is shared. As a result, the brain becomes fully engaged in a truly holistic manner.

> **Storytelling** can be used to teach or augment almost any topic using a variety of approaches. You can teach everything from history, to geology, to values. It is an especially good strategy for indirect instruction.

Storytelling can be used to teach or augment almost any topic using a variety of approaches. You can teach everything from history, to geology, to values. It is an especially good strategy for indirect instruction. Try having your students lay down on ground pads in sleeping bags while looking up at the stars during an "astro bivy." You can point out constellations while telling stories about the Greek myths associated with them. This approach to teaching is not only fun but can also bring your topic to life. Inevitably, students tap into their previous knowledge of Greek Mythology and share their stories with the group. This sharing of stories can then turn your class into a memorable and interactive shared learning experience.

Storytelling can also be used to introduce a historical event or help instill positive values. At some point, when teaching Leave No Trace minimum impact camping techniques, try telling the story of the Lorax by Dr. Seuss. This compelling story will encourage students to reflect upon their own values and actions. Following-up the story with a group *discussion* will help students process the information learned while offering an opportunity to transfer the knowledge gained to personal experiences in their own lives. When used this way, adding a story and a *discussion* can turn most topics into memorable experiences.

There is a special place for instructors to be the storytellers. Your own personal stories can be profound teaching tools especially if there is a clear message that others can benefit from. If your students have been struggling with the terrain, the bugs, or the cold weather, tell them a story about something that was truly difficult for you and emphasize how you grew from that experience. This can really be about grit. Throw in a transference piece so that students can get a glimpse into how we can all grow from tough experiences.

Another way to use stories is to examine the human condition while learning from others. Telling the amazing survival story of Ernest Shackleton's Trans-Antarctic Expedition, where his ship was crushed by ice, not only immediately warms up a group camping out in the cold, but also indirectly speaks volumes about the qualities of a good leader. In addition, telling stories of other cultures who have lived or traveled through areas that you are traveling through with students does wonders in bringing the landscape to life. Sharing stories of Cochise and the Apache people after a day of climbing in Arizona amidst the incredible mazes of rock at Cochise Stronghold is a truly memorable learning experience.

> There is a special place for instructors to be the storytellers. Your own personal stories can be profound teaching tools especially if there is a clear message that others can benefit from.

When students and instructors interact in a safe space and share stories on a personal level, the community grows stronger. As understanding grows, trust inevitably deepens, helping a group grow closer together. With a deeper understanding of each other growing, rapport deepens, and a stronger common group identity ultimately emerges.

Besides choosing the best story for the lesson that you want to teach, delivering that story can be an art in itself. There are unlimited ways of delivering a story, so you'll need to discover what works for you, your audience, and the type of story you are telling. Will you deliver your story in a conversational manner or a dramatic theatrical manner? Will you memorize your story or improvise? Will you be active and animated or subtle? Thinking through these scenarios will help you visualize the type of storyteller you want to be, and inevitably, the type of authentic, effective instructor you want to be.

Example: Caving - The Floyd Collins Story

After spending a bunch of time caving underground with your students and hooking your group on caving, share the story of Floyd Collins. He was a famous Kentucky caver who, while searching for another entrance to Crystal Cave, became trapped. Go into detail about the huge efforts that were made to save him, and the sad outcome that he ultimately did not survive.

Student Storytelling
Multi Oriented Teaching Strategy

Students can be really creative! The *student storytelling* strategy is fun because it fully engages the learner in the *storytelling* process. It offers students an opportunity to create stories and tell their own stories while empowering them to step into leadership, community building, and teaching roles.

Stories can be created or shared while traveling or sitting in camp. Along the trail, a wonderful way to get your students focused on the landscape and all of the little treasures along the journey is to start a story map. In the Aboriginal tradition, students work together (usually in groups no larger than 4), to "map" out their route. They create a story line and add the land features that they come upon to their story so that they can to retrace their steps if necessary, just like reading a map. Incidentally, this activity could work hand in hand with a map reading exercise. Students often create this type of story in song form to help with memorization. Student story maps also work quite well in caves when you want to encourage students to focus on the route in order to keep their bearings.

> Involving students in **storytelling** encourages creativity while empowering them to step into leadership, community building, and teaching roles.

Another *student storytelling* activity involves sitting around in a circle and creating an improvisational "traveling story." This is a classic teambuilding activity that starts with one person who says a word, sentence, or paragraph (depending on how you frame it), and then passes it on to the next person to add on to. Beyond teambuilding, student traveling stories ignite creativity while enhancing imagination and visualization skills. Listening skills are also honed when *storytelling* is incorporated into learning activities.

There is also much to be gained from creating a safe space for students to share their own stories. These can be funny, scary, personal, and meaningful stories. Set the stage according to your goals and the terrain you are traveling through. After a couple of days interacting with each other, have the group sit down together in a comfortable spot and share their fears, their hopes, and their dreams through story. This can also be revisited at any point throughout your journey.

In addition, you can encourage your students to share their own personal autobiographies by making time for one or two students to talk for a set amount of time during your evening gatherings. People tend to grow together much closer when they are given space to share. Prioritizing "air time" for students is invaluable.

Example: Story Song Map
This was created by second graders during an Australia study.

Our Walkabout Story Song
(An Aboriginal Inspired Map of our Journey). *Sung by our group and documented by Alexander.*

We're going on a walk
Through the big tall trees
We're going to discover
All kinds of new things

We're going on a hike
Through the portal of time
Next, we're going to do
The big penguin slide

Oh, we're going past the stump
Where we can fly
Now we're going down the hill
Where we can slip and slide

Oh, we're going past a rock
And a big huge tree
Then we take a big jump
Over the ice in the creek

We see our outdoor classroom
And the grandpa tree
We take a quiet moment
Just to stop and breathe

Then, we head up a hill
Where we see lots of tracks
Squirrel, rabbit, fox
Must have all had a blast!

Now it's time
To hike back to our room
And share our stories
Before we zoom!

Puppetry
Multi Oriented Teaching Strategy

A wonderful way to teach various outdoor education lessons is to use puppets. Especially with younger students, a hand puppet can quickly capture and retain attention. Puppets of all sizes and quality can be constructed or purchased at local bookstores, nature education centers, or online environmental education or teaching supply companies.

Mammal, bird, fish, reptile, amphibian, or insect puppets are especially stellar tools for teaching natural history lessons for the purpose of covering content knowledge or value-base topics. Soft and plush puppets can easily be carried on wilderness expeditions or in instructor daypacks. If kept hidden away until used, they make fun and memorable entrances into a lesson.

There are three principle teaching techniques available to you when using puppets. We call them: (1) Ventriloquist, (2) Translator, and (3) Sesame.

Ventriloquist

This *puppetry* technique requires you to perform your best character voice for the puppet by simulating the work of a ventriloquist. Of course, the majority of us cannot replicate the amazing skills of a professional ventriloquists without dedicating months or years of training, but we sure can all pretend to be one. A good trick for this technique is to place your puppet in front of your mouth when it is time for the puppet to talk. This way, the illusion is almost complete. Students will love watching you try to pull this off.

Translator

This technique is much easier than the previous one. The idea behind this technique is to introduce your puppet character as a very shy animal. In this scenario you ask questions to the puppet while the puppet gives you the answers to the questions by whispering in your ear, then "voilà" you interpret their answer using your own voice. You can also solicit questions from the audience to encourage interaction between your students and the character.

Sesame

This *puppetry* technique is the classic puppet show where the puppeteer is concealed behind an object. In an outdoor setting, you can easily create a blind by stretching a camping tarp between two trees. You can also hide inside a tent with your hand puppet sticking out of one of the doors, hide behind a tipped over canoe, or simply tuck yourself behind a large tree or a large rock.

Inspired by Sesame Street, this *puppetry* teaching technique may include two instructors, one hidden playing the character of the puppet and the other one acting as the host instructor interviewing or interacting with the puppet. You can also place more than one puppet behind your makeshift screen to allow interaction and dialogue between multiple puppet characters.

Example: Beaver Behavior

Scene set-up

The instructor sits in front of an upside-down canoe with a white board (i.e., plastic compactor trash bag) ready to teach about beaver behavior. The notes on the whiteboard about beavers and their behaviors are somewhat erroneous. For instance, one note says: "Beavers hibernate during the winter months."

As the instructor goes along introducing the topic for the lesson and explaining some of the facts written on the whiteboard, small wooden sticks get thrown at the instructor from the behind the canoe. Eventually, a loud voice rises from the back of the canoe stating: "*No – You are totally wrong!*" After this surprising interruption, a beaver puppet emerges from behind the canoe and a dialogue between the instructor and the puppet goes as follow:

Instructor: "What do you mean I am wrong?"
Puppet: "We don't hibernate, we are not marmots. We, Beavers remain active throughout the winter months."

Instructor: "How can you be active since the rivers, lakes and ponds, including beaver ponds, freeze over in the winter?"
Puppet: "We stockpile food for the winter near our beaver lodge."

Instructor: "Oh, is this the large pile of small trees and branches I often see in the water near your lodge in the fall?"
Puppet: "Yes, you got it! You have a good sense of observation for a biped."

The conversation between the instructor and the puppet continues with more back and forth questions and answers presenting correct facts about beaver behavior. Near the end of this impromptu interview with the puppet, the instructor can invite the students to ask questions to the guest puppet.

Student Puppetry
Multi Oriented Teaching Strategy

Another way to teach through *puppetry* is to have your students directly involved in creating their own puppet show. This teaching strategy is different from the previous one since it moves the level of student engagement from passive to active participation in the learning experience. Similar to having students create and present their own *skits* or role plays, *puppetry* by students is a great way to involve the learners with the subject via a fun and engaging medium.

Although it is possible for your students to use the ventriloquist, translator, or sesame *puppetry* techniques explained in the previous teaching strategy, the most appropriate technique for them is to use the classic French puppet theatre, where all of the puppeteers are behind a makeshift stage and manipulate the puppets in a comedy or dramatic short play.

Student puppetry moves the level of student engagement from a passive to an active participant in the learning experience.

This strategy works well if you subdivide your class into smaller groups of three to four students. Have the students pick some animal puppets, give them time to research the facts, concepts, or values they want to present, and create a short puppet show which can use comedic or dramatic interactions between their characters. In the backcountry, students can also turn their socks into puppets.

Having resources such as books, fact sheets, or internet access is essential for your students' content preparation. Of course, guidance from you could also be important during the puppet show preparation.

Once all of the groups have completed their preparations and perhaps rehearsed once, invite each team to present their puppet show.

Summarizing, through appropriate questioning, the highlights of the puppet shows' content after each presentation might also help assure that the appropriate facts, concepts, or values are understood and learned from the audience.

Example: Endangered and Threatened Species

Materials for Group 1:
Puppet of a Canadian Lynx, a snowshoe hare, and a person. Twigs that represent habitat and a paper "road."

Set-up
This first group of students can research and present a puppet show staring the threatened Canadian Lynx. The puppet show can showcase multiple threats that the Lynx faces and why it is considered threatened. When the show is finished, students can discuss the situation and reflect on possible action that can be taken to help the Lynx.

Break the rest of your group into small groups and follow this sequence with different threatened or endangered species. Close with a *discussion* that identifies common themes and challenges that different species face and ideas for action-oriented solutions.

Role-Play
Multi Oriented Teaching Strategy

Teaching through *role-playing* involves having the instructor give a small group of students a very specific scenario to act out that does not ask the students to improvise.

This strategy requires more prep on your part, but you as an instructor maintain control (for the most part) over what is being taught. The advantage of using this strategy over *skits* is that you avoid setting students up for failure by handing them a specific scenario (scene) to act out. Students are not expected to improvise, but rather be actors. The script is written, and they are the stars. You know what will be taught because you wrote the script.

This strategy helps eliminate instances of students coming up with *skits* that pass on incorrect information to their peers. When inaccurate information is passed on, it is much harder to re-teach accurate information to your group. *Role-playing* helps you avoid this pitfall.

There is definitely a place for both *role-playing* and *skits*, so choose your strategy based on your topic, goals, and objectives. During a short first aid scenario for example, you don't set students up to improvise their injuries, instead you tell them the specific symptoms that you want them to act out so that you can teach about a specific topic. However, if you want students to show the group highlights from their small group expedition, then improvised *skits* are perfect for sharing fun moments.

> In **role-playing**, instructors give students very specific scenarios to act out without improvisation. This strategy helps eliminate instances of students coming up with *skits* that pass on incorrect information to their peers.

Example: Minimize Campfire Impacts

A group of friends arrive at a campsite, Ana and Ahmed volunteer to set up the tents. Gianny works on getting water and staring dinner while Malik volunteers to collect wood and start a fire.

There are two fire rings at the campsite, one that is centralized and well establish – it has been there for years. There is even a forest service grill on it. The second fire ring is smaller, more recent and placed in a more fragile area with a much better view on the lake.

Malik choses to use the small fire ring.

When Gianny comes back with water from the lake, she notices that Malik is gathering wood around the small fire ring. Gianny asks Malik if he intends to use this site to make the fire. He says yes.

Confused, Gianny goes and talks with Ana and Ahmed about the site Malik chose for the fire. They all agree that they should let Malik know that the small fire ring should not be used. Gianny volunteers to talk with him. The conversation should go like this:

Gianny explains that the small fire ring is not an official fire site and that we should only use the large and older one.

Malik asks why and argues that the view is better here and less windy.

Gianny explains that creating multiple fire rings at one campsite is contrary to LNT principles, that we should minimize the impacts of campfires. Ideally, we should always concentrate the fire impact in one place if open fires are allowed.

Malik asks why this fire ring here is then.

Gianny explains it must have been someone who really did not know or may not have cared about LNT.

Malik suggest that perhaps they should remove the smaller fire ring and clean the site so that no other campers make the same mistake he was about to make.

Gianny agrees and says it is a great idea!

Theatrics
Multi Oriented Teaching Strategy

Teaching Through First Person Narrative

Theatrics can bring your lessons to life in a truly engaging and fun way! With this strategy you become an actor representing a real life or fictional character. You act as if you are this person, animal, or thing using first person dialogue. It can be even more effective if you dress up and use props that are relevant to your character and the time period while immersing yourself fully into your role.

To use this strategy, try to learn everything you can about your character and his or her world. You can even pick up an accent if appropriate. The key is to know enough about your person, animal, or thing to always stay in character while sharing accurate information. Be careful not to fall into the trap of making up your own information just to fill in the gaps. Anticipating questions that students will ask your character can help you prepare more thoroughly and allow you to answer the questions in a comfortable manner.

> When using the **theatrics** strategy, you become an actor representing a real life or fictional character.

Learning comes through the rich interaction between your character and your students. Your character can engage students both emotionally and cognitively by retelling current, historical, or even future events from a first-hand point of view. Principles of brain based natural learning support this strategy by pointing out that powerful learning is enhanced by rich emotional experiences which are guided by higher order functions.

Your character can facilitate *discussions*, invite questions, and even hold meaningful *demonstrations* for your students. In addition to wearing a costume and showing props, involving your audience's senses through touch, taste, and smell will help their brains process and retain this meaningful learning experience.

Imaginations will come to life as you bring Sir Edmund Hilary back from the past to tell about his early mountaineering days in

New Zealand and his climb to the top of Everest with Tensing Norgay. Impersonate a current climate scientist to explain your research on glaciers and global warming and how our environment is currently changing. Or, pretend that you are a robot from the future that has traveled back in time to tell humans about what has happened to the planet earth. The scenarios are endless, so be creative and your students will learn more than you could ever imagine.

Theatrics is also a strategy that is quite effective when used with other teaching strategies such as *storytelling* or *seeded questions*. Imagine dressing as John Muir and telling stories of living in Yosemite Valley and the heartbreak of losing the fight against damning the Hetch Hetchy River. Your character would bring the emotions felt over 100 years ago to life by allowing the students to interact with John Muir today.

While in character, you could engage students in discussing a topic that they may not know much about by planting seeded questions with them before class. During class, cue your students to ask your character these questions, then see how in-depth the learning can really go. See the section on *seeded questions* for more details on this strategy.

Example: Impersonate Jedediah Smith

Dress up and become Jedediah Smith, a famous hunter, trapper, fur trader, and early western explorer. Depending upon whether you are in the front country or the backcountry, you can really dress the part and even bring props and furs to show students while you tell stories of your mountain adventures and how you survived a bear mauling.

Instructor Impersonating Jedediah Smith

Skits
Multi Oriented Teaching Strategy

Skits are the opposite of role playing. In role playing, students follow a script and do not improvise. When teaching through *skits*, students are completely encouraged to improvise and be creative. *Skits* by definition are short comedy sketches or satires. They are designed to be fun and lighthearted. As a teaching tool, *skits* can entertain and engage students while delivering a message. The depth of the message, once again, depends upon your teaching objectives and how well your students are set up to deliver it.

As a teaching strategy, *skits* work well when they are used as part of a lesson. They are designed for situations when students will most likely come up with the answers, lessons, and actions that you want portrayed. Instead of writing a script, all that you need to do is come up with a scenario for the actors. You can verbally tell each group their scenario, or, if you plan ahead, you can hand them a sheet of paper describing their scenario in detail. The student actors will then take the liberty of coming up with the script, usually through improvisation.

Skits work well if students interpret your scenario in the manner that you intended. Depending upon the topic, if you want more control, write a more detailed scenario that you want the actors to follow. If you want to give the students more control, add less detail to your scenario.

Instructors can also be the actors in *skits*. In fact, it can be extremely fun for students to watch their instructors introduce concepts or values through *skits*. A skit can be used as a "hook" to pull your students into the lesson that you are about to teach, or they can be placed in the middle of a lesson when you want to demonstrate a topic such as the types of terrain and hazards that students may encounter. Instructors can take a serious group expedition behavior problem and act out a skit in front of everyone. By using humor, you can show how absurd a particular issue is through the use of a light-hearted skit followed by a deeper *discussion*. Although less engaging for students, when instructors become actors in *skits*, students inevitably have a fun and memorable learning experience.

In addition to being a wonderful teaching tool, remember that *skits* can also be used for fun and entertainment at the end of a long day. When groups play and laugh together, they typically develop a tighter and more memorable connection with each other. As an instructor, just make sure that you frontload a safe tone for the *skits*. Be careful that you do not let your safe learning environment slide away amidst the humor.

Example: Expedition Behavior with Winnie the Pooh

Character Traits

Pooh - Winnie the Pooh always means well, but often gets into trouble due to being too impulsive. He will literally do anything to get honey. His friendly nature is a wonderful trait, but his impulsiveness can be a problem especially when there is a limited amount of food on an expedition.

Piglet - Piglet is very anxious and lacks confidence. His judgement often gets skewed by his anxiety and the consequences at times affect others. This can impact an expedition in different ways.

Tiger - Tiger is always excited and full of energy. At times his hyper energy can be overbearing for others. This can be really fun, but also exhausting on an expedition.

Eeyore - Eeyore is nice, but he's always sad and pessimistic. He never has anything positive to say. This negative energy can get old and wear on others during an expedition.

Rabbit - Rabbit is high energy with great intentions, but he never relaxes. He is quite obsessive compulsive and overly concerned with having everything organized. This can play out in an interesting way on an expedition.

Owl - Owl is friendly and intelligent. Although bright, he lacks some common sense and therefore can send the group in the wrong direction at times.

Some Small Group Skit Ideas

It works well to have small group *skits* demonstrate a dysfunctional scenario first, and then flip the scene and demonstrate a highly functional group scenario during a second skit. These can be short (one - two minutes each).

- Winnie the **Pooh** obsesses about food in his cook group, honey in particular. Since he can't seem to get enough of it, he sneaks it during the night. Show how some other characters in his cook group respond. Flip (improve) the behavior for the second skit.

- When a hiking group gets into camp and finishes setting up tents and kitchen sites, they want to relax a little and rest their feet. **Rabbit** gets very annoyed with the "slackers" and pressures his tent group to line the food bags up in little rows and line boots up from largest to smallest, etc. (exaggerate orderliness). This does not go over well with the rest of the group. Flip (improve) Rabbit's behavior for the second skit.

- While hiking, some members of the group move at a slower pace. **Tigger** hops all around with an infinite amount of energy and pressures everyone the group to move faster. This becomes stressful for some. Show how the group responds to this intensity. Flip (improve) Tigger's behavior for the second skit.

- When hiking with **Owl**, have him recite facts about a specific plant or tree that are entirely false. Then have him tell the group exactly which way they need to go by looking at the map (which is actually the wrong way). The group listens intently and follows his lead. Show how the group responds once they figure out that they are lost. Flip (improve) Owl's behavior for the second skit.

Role Modeling
Multi Oriented Teaching Strategy

The *role modeling* strategy simply asks the instructor to role model skills or values that have been presented to the students. *Role modeling* can be effective in reinforcing desired student behavior. This may seem like an obvious strategy for instruction, but since it is not always the easiest strategy for instructors, it is important to include.

Whether you like it or not, students look to you as a role model. They will mimic your behaviors and values more than you know, so it's critical to personally demonstrate the behaviors that you want to instill in your students. Students learn from watching you be a good camper, a safe climber, an effective leader, or a positive expedition member. Students watch leaders so closely that they may pick up bad habits as well as good habits. Be hyperaware of your actions and how they may impact others. Instead of imposing your opinions and values on your students, try to present all sides of an issue and allow individuals a safe space for thinking critically on their own.

Example: Good Hygiene
After teaching students how to wash hands and brush teeth using minimum impact techniques, it's critical that you consistently role model washing your hands and brushing your teeth in this manner.

Discussion
Multi Oriented Teaching Strategy   LEVEL 5

Discussions work well when presented in either formal or informal ways. They are especially effective when discussing topics that are immediately relevant and meaningful to your students. When students have an emotional connection to a *discussion* topic, they generally become interested and engaged, thus allowing natural learning to take place.

This teaching strategy often begins with an instructor or student leader describing the goal or purpose of the group discussion. It can be initiated by posing an open-ended question or by reading a short article, poem or story. You can encourage students to participate in *discussions* by calling on them, passing around a "talking stick," or placing "*seeded questions*" among group members before the lesson begins.

> **Discussions** are most effective when sharing topics that are directly relevant and meaningful to your students.

In a formal *discussion*, you can frontload the actual *discussion* by assigning students to be "experts" or leaders for various parts of the dialogue. Prior knowledge of the topic can help students prepare for their "expert" roles in advance. This approach often has the advantage of leading to more lively and informed *discussions*.

Using this teaching strategy to inform your students about controversial issues can also be quite compelling. For example, discussing whether or not special backcountry areas should be published in magazines or protected from the hordes of readers who may want to travel to these areas can stir up a lively and educational *discussion*.

Informal *discussions* held in the evenings around a circle or campfire can also be extremely effective and memorable. After bushwhacking through a thick, old, clear-cut area on Forest Service Land, hiking past an open mine on BLM land, or encountering sheep or cattle in your camp, you can pull your group together for an informal *discussion* about land management. Capture the feelings of the group while the emotions of the day are still strong and begin sharing information about the multiple uses of government land. You could also turn the *discussion* into a formal class later that evening or allow the discourse to carry itself. If student interest is high, consider teaching an in-depth, hands-on lesson the next day using different teaching strategies that launch off the *discussion*. The fact that you already had the group reflecting on this issue through *discussion* will make their interest in the topic quite high since it is directly related to a recent experience.

Example: <u>Environmental Discussion Topics</u>
Land management issues
Local environmental issues
Global environmental issues
Climate Change issues

OUTDOOR EDUCATION TEACHING STRATEGIES

Debate
Multi Oriented Teaching Strategy

Debates offer a truly fun and engaging way for students to explore both sides of an issue in-depth while being challenged to think critically. This strategy requires the instructor to be organized with a well-structured plan that considers time, speaking guidelines, and closure. *Debates* are most effective when the issues are timely, relative, and of interest to your students.

Different organizational methods work better with different group sizes. If your student group consists of eight or less people, it may be beneficial to have one topic and then divide your group into the "pro" side and the "con" side of one issue. If you have more students, it works well to have more than one topic up for *debate* so that everyone involved has an opportunity to speak and give a rebuttal. Two to four people on one side of an issue works very well. The instructor typically acts as the moderator, vocalizing the time and guidelines.

For *debates* to be truly effective, it is necessary to either provide your students with information representing both sides of the issue or give them time to research their topics on their own in town before leaving. In order to fully prepare, it is important for students to thoroughly know both sides of the issue. In preparing this way, students will be better able to predict the arguments brought against their side and therefore be better equipped to come up with counter-arguments.

If students are passionate about one side of an argument, you could consider challenging them to take on the opposite side of the issue and research it in-depth. An incredible amount of learning can take place when we put ourselves in another's shoes.

It can also be quite effective to have an informal *debate* in which students team up according to their opinions on an issue. Granted, their arguments may be flawed a bit due to a lack of facts, but if you're in the middle of the woods having a hard time finding a good place to camp because huts have been placed in many of the good camping areas, then it may be an opportune time to have a *debate* about the pros and cons of backcountry huts.

Example: Debate Guidelines and Procedures
Tone: Be cordial, use active listening, and be respectful.
Participation: Everyone in your team must be an active participant in the *debate*.
Voice: Don't forget, this is a learning experience, not a tavern screaming match.
Supporting Evidence: Look for 4 to 5 points to support your position. Find valid sources (peer reviewed journals, books, third party research, etc.). Avoid blogs.

Example: Formal Debate Format
Opening statement (could be written) – 1 minute each side
Present your position – 1 - 5 minutes each side *(age dependent)*
Rebuttal – 5 - 10 minutes each side
Closing statement (could be written) – 1 minute each side
Open up to comments

Example: Debate Topics
Debate whether or not people should pay for their own rescue.
Debate the pros and cons of backcountry huts.
Debate the impact of using different technology in the backcountry.
Debate current land management issues affecting your students.

Example: Sources of Some Controversial Issues:

Controversial Issues in Adventure Education: A Critical Examination by Tom Potter and Scott Wurdinger (1999)

Controversial Issues in Adventure Programming by Bruce Martin and Mark Wagstaff (2012)

Exploratory Learning
Multi Oriented Teaching Strategy

Exploratory Learning is an incredibly subtle, yet effective teaching strategy. Bring your students to a creek, a pine forest, a bog or any not-too-fragile part of an ecosystem and back off while they play and explore on their own. This strategy is especially effective with younger students, but also helps to bring out the inner child in teens and adults by igniting a sense of wonder.

> The **exploratory learning** strategy involves stepping back and letting nature be the teacher.

It is amazing what students will do. Some will build and destroy mini damns to see the immediate results of their actions. Others will make a fort for squirrels out of sticks and leaves. Some may make a mud or sand pile and pour water on it to see it erode away. Still others may see a lake and decide that they want to make a raft out of dead wood and rope to see if it will float with someone on it (true story). In this situation, this "lazy" afternoon can quickly turn into a powerful opportune time for teambuilding.

Exploratory learning allows students to explore and interact with the natural environment on their own terms. When instructors make time and open the door for students to explore on their own, students consistently come up with fun, creative ways to interact with their environment. *Exploratory learning* is exciting, it encourages problem solving, and it is a powerful way of empowering students to connect authentically with the natural world.

It's important to set up guidelines before setting students off in the woods to wander around and explore. Set clear boundaries, including safety expectations around hazards such as water, tree climbing, etc. After setting up expectations, it's also helpful if you establish a distinct way to call your students back together. This makes regrouping so much easier.

As students return, you can bring the learning full circle by asking them to share what they were curious about and what they explored, saw, and experimented with. Facilitating a *discussion* at the end of the *exploratory learning* strategy opens the door for reflection, which helps solidify the learning and joy that takes place during this free-range learning.

One obstacle that may surface pivots around the different backgrounds of students. You may find that people who are accustomed to having every moment of their day filled with organized activities actually may not know how to "play" outdoors. First, they may just stand around looking awkward. We've seen this happen more frequently in recent years. Having students who are accustomed to playing outdoors draw them into their exploration, or *role modeling* exploring the outdoors yourself and having fun discovering new things is also a good way to pull them in.

So, when you are tempted to fill up every day with activities and lessons, just stop! Allow your students time to look, listen, and feel the place that they are passing through as visitors. They may discover more about the environment and themselves than you could ever "teach" them.

Example: Skipping Rocks

After arriving in camp and seeing flat rocks by the shore of the lake, put down your pack and start skipping rocks. Get excited about the skips and hand some rocks to your students if they don't immediately try skipping some on their own.

Socratic Method
Multi Oriented Teaching Strategy

The *Socratic Method* is a classic and often misunderstood teaching strategy in which the instructor asks a series of questions instead of just feeding information directly to students. In this method, there is an answer that you help the student discover within. You may not necessarily know the answer yourself, but you become a guide who prompts reflective thinking, recall, processing, and application.

Students search to discover the truth by thinking in-depth about the questions posed. When a contradiction is exposed, initial assumptions are proven false. This 7000-year-old teaching strategy is famous for developing critical thinking skills in students.

Asking students questions instead of handing them "truths" is a powerful way of empowering them to challenge themselves cognitively. Humans are curious by nature, so feeding this curiosity through questioning is quite effective. A growth mindset is encouraged when students are asked to think through questions and explain their reasoning. They often delve into deeper levels of thinking, sometimes get stumped, and then push past preconceived notions to understand concepts or solve problems.

In the outdoors, this teaching strategy works well when students work to understand abstract or scientific concepts. This strategy is very similar to *guided discovery*, but *guided discovery* works when students can actually see or touch something that they are being questioned about, while the *Socratic Method* asks students to think about more abstract questions and concepts.

Example: Socratic Questions

- How can we understand the concept of being a good steward toward the land?
- When can we justify anthropocentric (human centered) actions when making decisions?

Games
Multi Oriented Teaching Strategy

Games bring learning to life by tapping into the innate playfulness of learners. They inevitably act as effective metaphors for learning concepts, skills or values in a fun, interactive, and memorable way. Concepts can be reinforced using a game such as Jeopardy as an information review. Physical skills can be practiced using tag *games* such as canoe stroke tag in the water, and values can be put into action using a game such as a Leave No Trace scavenger hunt.

Games can be used to reinforce concepts, practice physical skills, or put values into action. They can also be played just for the fun of it!

Games of course should also be played just for the fun of it! No objective, no goals, just play because it is a really awesome and fun thing to do. We need that as humans! You may want to get a group to play an active game just to get them moving and burning energy before you refocus them onto another topic. In colder environments, active *games* can be used to rewarm students. The great thing about using *games* is that students inevitably bond while having fun together.

If your goal is to build a stronger sense of community within your group, using non-competitive teambuilding *games* can be extremely effective. Facilitating *games* that set students up to play together cooperatively can be quite positive. On the other hand, if your goal is to create a competitive environment, there may be a place for this, but be very careful with how you frame the competition. If you want to maintain a safe, positive, learning environment, only use competitive *games* if your group has reached an appropriate level of maturity, demonstrating that all members are highly supportive of each other. Beware if your group is still evolving, because competition may crush your safe learning environment.

How you frame a competition is also key. If you set it up as a fun and playful learning experience that de-emphasizes the competition, that's what it will be. If you set-it up to be a cut-throat game that focuses on winning, beware that the losers may not be happy afterwards and, if there is an educational objective, they may miss it. Just keep in mind the subtle influence that cooperative *games* and competitive *games* have on a group when choosing what route to take.

When designing *games* to match your learning objectives, consider using them as part of a lesson that incorporates multiple strategies. *Games* can be used to introduce a topic, create a fun hands-on activity during a lesson, or to assess knowledge gained at the end of a lesson. *Games* can also stand alone or serve as fun transitions or fillers. They can be designed to reinforce skills by creating rotating stations or "Skill Rodeos," or even "Olympic Events" that challenge students to demonstrate their newly acquired skills.

When facilitating *games*, don't forget to consider risk management. Safety of the students and care for the environment should all be looked into before starting. Choose a location that is suitable for your activity. If you want students to run, make sure that the terrain is suitable for running. If it is not, adapt your game or chose another game that can be played safely at the site, or if possible, at another nearby site. Even a simple game of hacky sack played on rocky or uneven terrain can lead to a severe ankle sprain and evacuation. Before setting your game into action, set clear guidelines and boundaries for safe play. It especially helps to brief your students on the reasons why safety is so important. Are you 20 miles from a trailhead? Ask the students what an evacuation would entail? Involving students in your decision-making will help instill sound judgment while expanding their own risk management skills.

Example: Compass Course Challenge

At the end of a class on how to use a compass, break students into small groups and get them excited about participating in a Compass Course Challenge. Before class, set up at least one full course (10 bearing points) for every four students in your group and have the courses go off in different directions. This takes a bit of time, so plan ahead.

It's ideal but just not practical to set up a different compass course for every two students. Even though they are in groups of four, students should work with a partner and have one compass between the two of them so that they are able to take turns setting the bearing and following it together. It's important that everyone has an opportunity to touch the compass and adjust the bearing multiple times.

When setting up the course, try placing flagging tape behind the tree or rock that you are setting the bearing to. On this tape, use a permanent marker to write the next bearing that the students should set on their compass and how many strides they will need to take to reach the next point.

Before starting, demonstrate the difference between a step and a stride. A complete stride is actually two steps (left foot and right foot forward). Explain that you set the course stride numbers based on your stride length. At this point have everyone practice walking and counting strides with you while getting a sense of how their personal stride may differ slightly from yours (depending on leg length).

Once students understand the challenge of finding all of the bearing points, build up the excitement and send them off. If you want to really make your students happy, give them a candy prize at the end of the course. This is a no fail hit!

Problem Solving Activities
Multi Oriented Teaching Strategy **LEVEL 5**

Problem solving activities present a perfect strategy for challenging students to work together, think creatively, and focus on accomplishing a task. Like *games*, *problem solving activities* function well on their own or when incorporated with other strategies in a lesson.

To use this strategy, the instructor creates a challenge or problem that needs to be solved. It can be either an individual or group challenge that entails real or perceived risk depending upon your situation and objectives. For this strategy to work, it is important to ensure that the students already have some prior knowledge or skills that will enable them to solve the problem at hand. As an instructor, depending on the group and the situation, you may want to set students up for success, or choose to allow them to struggle, missing the target and reflecting on how to work together in the future to be successful.

> **Problem solving activities** present a perfect strategy for challenging students to work together, think creatively, and focus on accomplishing a task.

Maybe your students are learning to travel off-trail while working on map reading and route-finding skills. Instead of pointing out the route that you would choose to take based on the map and terrain, put the challenge to the group to find the best route based on the information they currently have. The problem-solving lesson can continue throughout the day as they navigate through the terrain, assessing their plan and changing it if necessary, based on the new information at hand.

As an instructor, you can take on the role of a consultant, offering insights when students ask or when a teachable moment arises. If a group "cliffs out," they will soon learn the hard way that they have to backtrack and find an alternate route that isn't as steep that they can safely navigate. Travel days offer endless opportunities to teach students hands-on skills through problem solving.

You could also set-up a contrived challenge that gets your group working together while refining skills. At camp, have the group set up three totally different bear hang systems while being timed to see how well they understand the principles, systems, and knots used. Or, after teaching a Tyrolean traverse over a small creek, you could use the problem-solving strategy as a tool for refining skills. Challenge your group to rebuild the complete Tyrolean system, send a person across the creek, and then reverse it to the other side within a certain amount of time. Since the use of this system is only needed under somewhat extreme conditions, learning and practicing the skills first in a contrived setting can prove to be extremely educational and fun!

> Travel days offer endless opportunities to teach students hands-on skills through problem solving.

In addition to backcountry *problem solving activities*, there are countless team-building activities that you can challenge your group to solve problems with. Tie a rope between two trees (just below waist level) and ask your group to get from one side of the rope to the other without going under or around. You can even build up an exciting story or scenario to make it more fun! Dial in on the potential hazards in the area that you choose to use (such as uneven terrain, rocks, etc.) and adjust your site as needed. As with most challenges, be sure to set up safety guidelines.

One other use for the problem-solving strategy is assessment. You can set up a problem that needs to be solved as a way to assess student's

> Another use for the problem-solving strategy is assessment. You can set up a problem that needs to be solved as a way to assess student's knowledge and skills.

knowledge and skills. If you want to know how well students understand how to use a GPS, set-up a scavenger hunt challenge with waypoints that need to be found. Partners will need to work together to find all of the points while demonstrating their knowledge of how to use a GPS.

After students participate in a problem-solving challenge, it is important to end the process by reflecting on the challenge as a group. The experiential learning cycle really isn't complete until students are able to reflect on what they did and transfer their learning so that they can apply it to future situations.

Example: Stove Repair Challenge

Challenge students to practice stove repair by secretly taking a piece out of each group stove (such as a jet or fuel line), and asking students to determine if something is broken, clogged or missing.

Simulation
Multi Oriented Teaching Strategy

A *simulation* is the closest teaching strategy to mimic an actual event. It typically proceeds in real time within a real environment, giving students an opportunity to apply new skills while analyzing situations and coming up with creative solutions. *Simulations* take students to the highest level of Dale's Cone of Experience by putting them in situations that ask them to solve problems.

Simulations offer safe spaces for students to practice applying first aid skills, search and rescue skills, leader-of-the-day skills, and more. Due to the experiential nature of a *simulation*, think about setting aside a significant amount of time for it to be truly effective. Some first aid *simulations* may last for a few minutes to a few hours while something such as a cave search and rescue *simulation* could take all day.

Completing the experiential learning cycle with a reflection piece makes this strategy fully effective. Asking students to share their insights on what went well and what could be improved provides a tremendous area for growth. Some instructors give real-time feedback during the scenario, others hold feedback until the *simulation* is complete and then share insights individually and with the group during a reflection period. In the end, the learning curve is quite steep when you give students the freedom to tackle real-world challenges experientially through *simulations* and reflection.

Example: Different Simulation Scenarios Based on Time

- Simple first aid situation (30-minute simulation)
- First aid with evacuation (1/2-day simulation)
- Cave search and rescue (1-day simulation)
- Natural history wolf pack (24-hour simulation)

Solo Experience
Multi Oriented Teaching Strategy

The use of a *solo* is a compelling teaching strategy that can be effectively used to practice skills and reflect upon learning. The role of the instructor prior to the *solo* is to set goals, plan, motivate, and prepare students for the event.

Depending on the type of course that you are running, you may design a *mini-solo* that lasts from one hour to one half day. Longer *solos* can run from one day to 24 hours or more and may include keeping students out on their own overnight.

Your organization should create a set of risk management protocols to follow to ensure the safety of all individuals. The level of preparation needed for students is often directly related to the length or conditions of the *solo* environment. Make sure that your students are adequately prepared both mentally and physically.

Giving students choices while setting up the *solo* will help to motivate and empower them. Some areas for choice include the level of aloneness preferred, which is really the level of interaction with the instructor who checks-in on them. The remoteness from the instructor's site can also be turned into a choice depending upon the age and maturity of the students. Whether or not students would like to try fasting could also be turned into a choice if the conditions, preparation, and course type allow for this.

> The role of the instructor prior to the **solo** is to set goals, plan, motivate, and prepare students for the event.

Solos are effective learning opportunities for a number of reasons. Historically, a specified time spent alone in the wilderness was considered a rite of passage for many cultures. Today, because students are caught up in a busy world and possibly even a busy course, giving them time to just sit alone and listen to nature along with their inner thoughts can be a wonderful gift. It is such a rare concept in today's world that even a half-hour or one-hour *solo* can have positive, memorable effects on students.

To help students pull meaning out of the experience, you can have them write a letter to themselves, draw, or answer questions that you posed to them before the *solo*. *Solo* time alone will also give students an opportunity to assess their own intrapersonal and technical skills before they rejoin the group. When framed well, *solos* are almost always a highlight.

After the *solo*, you can welcome students back into the group with a celebration (potluck dinner, pancake breakfast, twiggy fire cake, treats, etc.). You can also set-up a formal or informal ceremony that helps students share and reflect upon their *solo* with the group. This is the time when students can share their drawings, writings, thoughts, and accomplishments with the group. Processing the *solo* in this manner is essential in helping students pull more meaning out of the experience and transfer the learning back into their lives when they return home.

Example: <u>Different Solo Experiences Based on Time</u>

- Mini-solos (Typically 1 - 2 hours)
- Time Choice Solos (Give students a choice between a 4, 6, or 12-hour solo.)
- Overnight Solos (Students spend 1 night on their own.)
- Multi-day Solos (These typically run 2 to 5 days)

Peer Teaching
Multi Oriented Teaching Strategy

Peer teaching empowers students to improve their leadership skills by stepping into the role of the instructor. For *peer teaching* to be successful, you need to set the peer teachers up for success. One approach is to begin by thoroughly teaching a specific skill, piece of information, or a value to a small group of students. These students then become the "specialists" who teach the same lesson to another small groups of students.

If you have students who already know the skill that you want to teach, meet with them ahead of time to make sure that they really do know the skill well enough to teach it accurately. If you are teaching a group how to tie a bowline, first try demonstrating how to tie the bowline to the group, and then break into smaller groups, each with a competent peer leader who can re-teach the skill one-on-one. It's crucial that you prepare your peer leaders well so that wrong information or sloppy skills are not taught to the group. By first demonstrating the skill yourself, you plant the seed for accuracy from the onset.

If you have two instructors, it also works well to empower the entire group to take on peer leadership roles. Each instructor can teach a skill to half of the group. Once all of the students understand and are competent with sharing knowledge, values, or skills, have them pair up and teach each other what they learned.

There is the potential for information to be lost whenever you hand the teaching over to students, however, it is also a powerful tool for learning, so you can always bring the group back together at the end for a closure piece. In doing this you can make sure that students learned exactly what they were supposed to learn.

Example: Topics That Work Well with Peer Teaching
Natural history topics
Knots
Cooking or baking a specific meal or treat

Service Learning
Multi Oriented Teaching Strategy **LEVEL 8**

The *service learning* strategy can be truly effective because it integrates meaningful community service activities with instruction and reflection. It enriches learning experiences, teaches civic responsibility, and ultimately strengthens not only communities, but also student groups.

Students are able to work with real people to solve real-life problems while putting to use either previously learned or newly acquired skills. Because our search for meaning is innate, *service learning* is an extremely powerful teaching strategy. Students often comprehend more effectively when they are engaged in meaningful learning activities. There is also typically an emotional element to *service learning* that helps make the learning more memorable.

> Because our search for meaning is innate, **service learning** is an extremely powerful teaching strategy. Students often comprehend more effectively and develop an emotional connection with a project when they are engaged in meaningful **service learning** activities.

Service learning projects can be impromptu or pre-planned. Impromptu projects are basically teachable service moments. Imagine that your students are hiking through a wilderness area when they come upon a fire ring that some hikers illegally built next to a pond. This is a perfect opportunity to review Leave No Trace principles with students along with Forest Service Wilderness area regulations. After sharing and discussing these insights and frontloading the idea that it really doesn't belong there, frame a question to students about what they think your group should do next. As an instructor, if you frame a service choice effectively, students will almost always want to help.

Orchestrating a successful pre-planned *service learning* project can take some serious preparation. First determine the goal of your project and then calculate the approximate duration time. Will this last for one hour, one day, or an entire course? Depending upon the size of your project, you may need to tap into other resources such as your administration, the Forest Service, or any other community or government agencies that you think need to be involved. After meeting with these players, determine the scope of the project along with the equipment and the resources needed. A big recommendation is to ask for help. *Service learning* projects can grow bigger than you initially planned, so having a strong support network can be critical.

Involving students in as much planning, skill development and leadership as possible can definitely help to steepen their learning curve. Instruction on this level may come mostly through coaching and guiding students as you empower them to take on new roles. Throughout the *service learning* project, it is also important for you to be right in the mix, helping and supporting students as the project moves forward.

After the activity or project is finished, pulling it all together through reflection is critical to compete the learning process. You can frame the reflection in many different ways. You may want to have the group discuss the project or write or draw about their experiences. They could point out the highs and lows or share the most important thing that they learned from participating in the activity. Guided reflection is really important for turning a simple service project into a *service learning* project.

Example: Service Learning Applications

Impromptu: Campsite clean-up, dismantling fire rings that don't meet regulations

Planned: Trail restoration, tree planting, bridge building, dismantling old shelters or bridges, making Jr. Naturalist Booklets for an area

CHAPTER 5

Assessment

Why Assess Students

Assessing Student Learning

Assessing Student Skills

Assessing Student Content Knowledge

Assessing Student Values

Why Assess Students

A Rational for Assessment

Should I Assess Student Learning?

Since many outdoor educators are not required to give formal grades, the thought of assessing is commonly lost. But it's important to distinguish between assessing and grading. Grading is not the same as assessment. It is a byproduct.

If you are instructing, assessment is a critical part of the learning loop. First you identify your learning objectives, then you consider your group and the environment that you are teaching in, next you come up with strategies to instruct and formatively assess along the journey (revising your strategies as needed), and lastly after teaching you assess what your students have learned. Without completing the loop, you miss knowing if your instruction was effective and if your students actually learned what you sought out to teach.

> Any time you are instructing, remember that assessment is a critical part of the learning loop.

As an instructor, it is critical to do some form of assessment to inform your teaching so that you can continually challenge your students to excel.

Assessing Student Learning

Formative Assessment vs. Summative Assessment

Formative Assessment

Formative assessment can occur on a day-to-day basis throughout a course and works best if it is part of the instruction itself. Formative assessment is used to monitor student learning by checking frequently for understanding. This type of assessment provides ongoing feedback that can be used by instructors to track the effectiveness of their teaching so that they can adapt, individualize, and focus their instruction. The information obtained from this type of assessment can help instructors modify instruction as they teach to make their lessons more effective. Research has identified formative assessment as being critical in student improvement.

A perfect example of applying this form of assessment when teaching technical skills is by using the teaching strategy *EDP-ECP* (Explain, Demonstrate, Practice – Evaluate, Correct, Practice). It is not enough to simply explain, demonstrate, and ask students to practice a skill. The deeper, more focused learning comes when instructors watch students practice and then evaluate, immediately correct any errors, and ask the students to practice again. It would be very difficult for students to learn how to tie knots, for example, if the instructor asked them to practice tying knots but neglected to provide any immediate feedback.

A classic example of formatively assessing content knowledge occurs when playing a game of natural history Jeopardy. After students learn about different animals that inhabit the region you are traveling through, either from "nature nuggets" spread out over a week, or a more focused class, it can be fun to check for retention and understanding by playing a silly game such as Jeopardy. Students have fun playing this game while you get insights into what they really know and understand.

Formative assessments not only help instructors identify where students are struggling, but also give students a realistic idea of areas of strengths and areas to work on. Through formative assessments, students can actively assess their own performance and the performance of their peers in a supportive learning community. The beauty of formative assessment is that in addition to helping the instructor know where to modify lessons to meet student needs, it also strategically places the emphasis on learning, not performing, which inevitably feeds intrinsic motivation.

Example: <u>Formative Assessment of Different Areas</u>

Skills:
- Formal and informal observations
- Games
- Small and large group challenges
- Partner sharing and adapting
- Friendly contests
- EDP - ECP

Content Knowledge:
- Discussions
- Questions
- Written responses
- Games
- Skits
- Mini quizzes
- Projects
- Mapping
- Modeling

Value:
- Focused discussions
- Questions
- Demonstrations
- Written reflections
- Skits
- Debates
- Partner sharing
- Group sharing

Summative Assessment

Summative assessments are usually given at the end of a class, workshop, or course, and evaluate student learning against established benchmarks. A summative assessment is basically a measure of what a student has learned, demonstrated, and retained. This type of assessment usually occurs too late in a course to rectify instruction but can be used to guide instructor recommendations and next steps for students.

Summative assessments are often linked to an evaluation and therefore typically provide students with extrinsic motivation for improvement. At times, students are just passively involved learners receiving information about their performance when it is too late to change. However, if summative assessments are given periodically throughout the course, students may have an opportunity to act immediately upon the feedback.

Example: Summative Assessment of Different Areas

Skills:
- Demonstration
- Performance
- Peer teaching

Content Knowledge:
- Higher level questioning
- Problem-solving
- Concept application

Value:
- Action / behavior
- Written reflection
- Group discussion

Assessing Student Skills
Giving Constructive Feedback

Feedback is essential in assessing student skill development. There are three key components of effective feedback: timeliness, specificity and positive framing. For feedback to be relevant and effective, it is best if it comes directly after a student tries a skill or is formatively assessed on content knowledge. Specific, timely feedback can make a huge impact if it focuses first on specific positive praise and proper performance, and then asks the student to self-critique before specific feedback for improvement is given. This approach feeds a growth mindset and typically motivates a student to work hard.

Constructive feedback often addresses the emotional (affective) domain and the performance-based (effective) domain. Feedback hitting the emotional domain puts the focus on effort, while feedback hitting the performance-based domain moves the focus to the skill or content knowledge performance. Ultimately, it is preferable and more effective to blend emotional and performance-based feedback together. The sandwich approach of placing critical feedback between two positive pieces can be helpful, but it is over simplified so try to consider all key components when giving feedback.

> Specific, timely feedback can make a huge impact if it focuses first on specific positive praise for effort and proper performance, and then asks the student to self-critique before you pass on specific feedback for improvement.

For a student to actually internalize feedback, it is critical to create a positive, non-threatening course culture that supports the emotional domain. Building a culture that values learning by improving from mistakes can help set students up with a growth mindset that is open to feedback. With this level of instructor and group support, it is easier for a student to swallow constructive feedback, especially when the focus is first on effort and positive growth, and then on overcoming mistakes.

Assessing Student Skills

If you are assessing a student's skill performance through one-on-one feedback and have already given specific positive feedback on effort, it is helpful to pose questions that indirectly ask a student to self-evaluate. "How did it go for you?" "What do you think went well?" "What do you think you are mastering now?" Focus on the positive effort first, and then see if the student can self-critique. If he or she is unable to come up with something to improve upon, then step in as needed and give specific feedback for improvement.

It is quite helpful to assess student skills by breaking feedback down into manageable pieces or digestible "chunks." In this approach, you give a student only one piece of feedback to work on at a time. After the student has shown improvement in this specific area, if needed, repeat the feedback cycle with the next chunk to work on. Feeding students multiple chunks of feedback at one time can be overwhelming and discouraging, especially when learning a new skill. Although sticking to one chunk may seem slow, it can go a long way in moving a student forward.

> **Self-reflection Questions**
>
> After giving a student specific positive feedback on effort, it is helpful to pose the following types of questions that indirectly ask a student to self-evaluate.
>
> "How did it go for you?"
>
> "What do you think went well?"
>
> "What areas do you think you are mastering now?"

Example: Gradient of Effective Feedback

Trap Feedback
"Hey good job, but I noticed that you should really improve the way that you rotate your body."

The focus here is on specific improper performance, but feedback on good performance is vague. It is very important to give specific feedback on effort and feedback for skills done well.

OK Feedback
"Hey, great job on the j-stroke, but make sure that during the recovery phase, you take the time to really recover your stroke."

This is timely, but vague positive feedback. The focus is still on bad performance.

More Effective Feedback
"Alex, great effort on your J-stroke. I see you putting in a lot of focused time with hard work. I especially like the work of your upper hand throughout the whole catching and power phase of the stroke. However, what do you think happens to your upper hand during the recovery phase of the stroke? If you haven't noticed, your thumbs keep pointing down so that your blade doesn't feather during the recovery phase."

The feedback is not only timely, but it puts a heavy focus on specifically pointing out effort and what a student is doing well. This positive and specific approach helps build the student's confidence and indirectly feeds motivation to continue trying. Next, this approach asks the student to self-critique in order for you to formatively assess awareness of the skill. Finally, if the student doesn't understand what he or she needs to improve upon, then specific feedback is given for improvement.

Peer and Group Feedback

Although feedback is often targeted at an individual, it is also effective to utilize peer or group strategies. If you are teaching a skill and see a pattern of constant errors within your group, this may reflect a hole in your teaching that needs to be addressed. Stopping the entire group and re-teaching a component or giving specific feedback to everyone at the same time can nip big errors quickly.

You can also address the whole group to positively reinforce the emotional (affective) domain. "Hey everybody, I see some great effort being put forth here. People are trying very hard to learn how to tie a figure 8 follow-through. Keep it up!" Then walk around giving specific feedback. If some students in the group seem to grasp the skill sooner than others, try differentiating by saying, "If you have tied this knot three times properly, fully dressed and set, try it a few more times with your eyes shut." You can also ask students who have grasped a skill to give some tips to peers who may be struggling. These strategies often help engage and hold interest within your group since students typically pick-up skills at different rates.

When giving technical skill feedback, after seeing one person doing something wrong, try to avoid the trap of stopping the entire group and correcting everyone by pointing out what one person was doing wrong. This not only embarrasses the student who was corrected, but it wastes time since other students may not have needed the same specific feedback.

Finally, if you do choose to use peer feedback, don't assume that students know how to give effective feedback. Feedback can be quite subjective, so giving students the tools to be positive, tactful, and objective is important.

> If you are teaching a skill and see a pattern of constant errors within your group, this may reflect a hole in your teaching that needs to be addressed.

Remember that giving feedback is a skill. Without a doubt, students will benefit from learning and practicing how to give feedback under your guidance.

Assessing Student Content Knowledge
The Art of Questioning, Bloom's Taxonomy

Bloom's revised taxonomy includes remembering, understanding, applying, analyzing, evaluating, and creating.

Depending on the nature of your topic, the time allotted, and the goals of your lesson, you can choose the level of depth at which you want to assess your students.

Content knowledge lessons could include natural science topics such as weather, geology, local species, tracking, plant identification, ecosystems, astronomy, mountain ecology, history of the area, etc. It can also include many first aid classes and leadership models & theories.

To be effective, assessing content knowledge typically requires a different approach than assessing skill development. You can get insight into the level of student understanding by involving students in discussing, writing, playing *games*, performing *skits*, mapping, modeling, creating projects, questioning, and more.

Bloom's Taxonomy, which was revised by Anderson & Krathwohl in 2001, is an excellent tool for assessing students through the use of question prompts. It begins with a basic level of recall and deepens to challenge students to combine concepts and parts of knowledge to come up with new ideas or items.

The revised taxonomy includes: remembering, understanding, applying, analyzing, evaluating, and creating. Depending upon the nature of your topic, the time allotted, and the goals of your lesson, you can choose the level of depth that you want to assess your students on at any given time. You could also start with basic questions and progress to more in-depth ones.

Blister Prevention and Care

If you are teaching students how to prevent and take care of blisters, you may want to formatively assess their comprehension by asking questions that begin with the basics.

Remember

For example, see what the students **remember** by asking them to "describe what happens when there is friction between your boot and your heel?"

Understand

If they remember, then take it to the next level by testing their **understanding**. Try asking, "What could happen if you ignore a hot spot when it is forming?"

Apply

If it is clear that your students understand the process, see if they can **apply** this knowledge in a new way. Ask, "What actions would you take if you feel a hot spot forming?"

Analyze

If students take a clever action, continue taking your formative assessment to the next level of **analyzing**. "If a hot spot has already turned into a flat, early-stage blister, what are the problems that could arise out of simply applying moleskin to the surface? How could you avoid these problems?" Questions can actually be part of your lesson with formative assessment built in.

Evaluate

Next, you can see if students can justify their treatment decision by having them **evaluate** their plan. "What choice would you have made if the blister was already filled with fluid and was about to pop?"

Create

Finally, try moving the questions into **creating**. "Your challenge is to devise a way to help keep the blister from growing and getting infected."

The above example shows teaching and assessment questions that progress through each stage of Bloom's Revised Taxonomy question prompts. Below see the categories and question prompt ideas that you can apply to just about any area of content knowledge that you want to teach and assess.

Remembering (Can a student recall or remember information?)
   Question Prompts:
   What do you remember about…?
   How would you define…?
   Describe what happens when…?
   What does it mean…?
   How…?
   Who…?
   Why…?
   When…?

Understanding (Can a student comprehend and explain ideas or concepts?)
   Question Prompts:
   How would you clarify the meaning…?
   What would happen if…?
   What did you observe…?
   How would you compare…?
   How would you contrast…?
   What can you infer from…?
   How can you describe…?
   Give an example…

Applying (Can a student apply information in a new way?)
   Question Prompts:
   How would you develop…?
   How would you change…?
   How would you demonstrate…?
   How would you determine…?
   What actions would you take to perform…?
   Predict what would happen if…
   What is another way you could choose to…?

Analyzing (Can a student break down ideas into parts and draw connections among ideas?) Ask students why they chose a certain problem solving technique and why it worked.
 Question Prompts:
 What is the function of...?
 What are the pros and cons of...?
 How can you compare the different parts...?
 How would you explain...?
 What can you point out about...?
 What is the problem with...?
 Why do you think...?

Evaluating (Can a student justify a decision?)
 Question Prompts:
 What criteria would you use to assess...?
 What choice would you have made...?
 What is the most important...?
 What is your opinion of...?
 What consistencies and inconsistencies appear?
 Which is more important?
 Which is more appropriate?
 What information would you use to prioritize...?
 What would you suggest...?

Creating (Can a student combine elements into a new whole, create a new product, or come up with new ideas for new situations?)
 Question Prompts:
 What alternative would you suggest for...?
 What changes would you make to revise...?
 How would you explain the reason...?
 How would you generate a plan to...?
 What facts can you gather...?
 What would happen if...?
 Devise a way to...
 How would you improve...?

You can use these types of question prompts as formative and summative assessments to help you focus on where to direct your feedback or redirect your teaching. Follow the same feedback loop that is used with assessing a skill but adapt it more to the levels of Bloom's Revised Taxonomy depending upon the depth that you are seeking from students.

Example: Using Bloom's Revised Taxonomy for a Lightning Class

Creating	How would you generate a plan to...
Evaluating	What information would you use to prioritize...
Analyzing	Why do you think certain areas in the mountains are safer than others during a thunderstorm?
Applying	How would you determine where to place your group during a thunderstorm?
Understanding	What would happen if the ground becomes negatively charged?
Remembering	Can anyone describe what happens when cumulonimbus clouds move over an area?

Assessing Student Values

Reflective Assessment

Assessing student values can seem quite subjective, but by using the *Socratic Method*, you can objectively survey what students think and feel on a variety of topics. This type of questioning does not pass judgement, but instead allows you to assess a student's ability to express themselves, their value positions, and where their thinking may be clear or foggy.

According to master outdoor educator Clifford Knapp, you can prepare for this type of questioning by predicting issues that may arise from a lesson or activity and then write relevant questions for each one in advance. Students can reflect on values by sharing thoughts verbally, through writing or drawing in personal or group journals, by expressing themselves through *visual imagery*, reflecting on *quotes*, *readings*, or *case studies*, and by reflecting on *nature awareness activities*.

You could even predict different student responses to your questions and prepare follow-up questions in advance. Since it is impossible to fully predict the direction that will emerge out of student *discussions*, being able to read a group and spontaneously come up with questions to guide a *discussion* is a valuable skill to develop.

One of the worst responses a student can make to a value-based question posed by you is, "I don't know." This is basically direct feedback from the student implying that you really need to go back and reframe or reteach the topic at hand. Clearly the students aren't fully engaged or authentically challenged if they are able to shut down in this manner. Rethinking your approach is worthwhile.

Example: Leave No Trace Personal Ethics Class

One goal of teaching a Leave No Trace personal ethics class it to empower students to think through their own actions in order to begin making decisions about their personal impact on the Earth.

For example, in addition to thinking about why it may be important to respect wildlife in the backcountry, you could transfer the question to habits back home in order to challenge and assess their thought process. You may start by saying that some people love to feed birds in the winter with a birdfeeder. In fact, there is an international bird count that you can be a part of by observing birds and tallying those that come to your feeder in the winter.

Now start the assessment process by asking students what they think of the action of people feeding wild animals in the winter. This could lead to a lively *discussion*. Next ask students to think about what they would each do and why. Explore how far they will go with personal decisions.

After the *discussion*, you can solidify this assessment by asking students to write down what they would personally do in this situation and why. This should not only help them clarify their own values, but it will also give you even deeper insights into their thinking.

Appendix

Sample Lesson Plans

Lesson Plan Preface

Lesson Plan for Teaching a Technical Skill

Lesson Plan for Teaching Content Knowledge

Lesson Plan for Teaching Values

Teaching Resource

Outdoor Teaching Strategy Field Guide

Lesson Plan Preface

The following sample lesson plans are quite detailed. They are intended to give you an idea of the depth that goes into a well thought out lesson and the multiple teaching strategies that can be applied. New instructors or instructors teaching a topic for the first time will absolutely benefit from writing detailed plans.

More experienced instructors will always benefit from thinking through their lessons but may be able to pull them off with little to no writing. Challenge yourself! If you are super experienced and teach all of your lessons the same way year after year, step out of your comfort zone and try applying some new strategies. Take a risk! We ask our students to take risks regularly.

We chose the following sample lesson plans as a guide, but the exact format you choose to use is obviously up to you or your program. The important thing to remember is to include or at least think through these key planning items:

Planning and Preparation
Lesson Plan Title
Educational Goals
Educational Objectives
Student Preparation (background knowledge & materials)
Instructor Materials
Preparation
Duration
Location
Foul Weather Alternative

Lesson Content and Methods
Creative Opening "Hook"
Body of Instruction
    Outline
    Lesson strategies with details
Closure

Evaluation
Evidence of Student Learning

Sample Lesson Plan for Teaching a Technical Skill

Instructor(s): Julie & Christian

I. Planning & Preparation

A. **Lesson Plan Title:** Making Your Home Away from Home

B. **Educational Goals:** To help students develop the skills required to use a tarp to build an effective outdoor shelter.

C. **Educational Objectives:** Students will be able to...
   1. Accurately explain the advantages and disadvantages of nylon and silicone coated tarps.
   2. Accurately explain the principles related to the proper set-up of a ridge line, sidewalls and corners
   3. Successfully use a ground stake.
   4. Successfully build an "A-frame" shelter using natural anchors for the ridge line.
   5. Successfully build a "lean-to" shelter using two natural anchors for the ridge line and two hiking or natural poles.
   6. Successfully build a "flat top" shelter using two or more natural anchors.

D. **Student Preparation:**
   Student Background Knowledge:
   1. Students should have already learned the following knots: truckers hitch, clove hitch and bowline.
   2. Students should know how to carefully select an appropriate campsite.

   Student Materials Needed:
   1. Bug net (anticipate distracting mosquitoes)
   2. Rain gear (as needed)

E. **Instructor Materials Needed:**
   - 3 silicone coated nylon tarps with ropes
   - 1 nylon tarp
   - 24 tent pegs
   - 6 ski poles

F. **Duration:**
   1 Hour

G. **Location:**
   Open Forest – Langdon Woods

H. **Foul Weather Alternative:**
   In case of rain, make sure that everyone has appropriate rain gear. If too windy, use a more appropriate location.

II. Lesson Content and Methods

A. **Creative Opening "Hook":**
   Put the tips of your fingers together so that your hands create an inverted "V" position to create a pointy roof over your head. Wait for a little while until all of your students are looking at you in puzzlement. Then, with the strongest conviction, explain that this sign is the "International sign for shelter" and that if you use it, people anywhere in the world will understand that you are looking for a shelter... or that you are possibly looking for a diving cliff, or a pointy hat, or that you are the member of the "Secret Order of the Pyramid Keepers."

B. **Body of Instruction:**
   <u>Lesson Outline</u>

   1. Tarp Fabric (i.e., material)
   2. Tarp Dimension
   3. Tarp Set-up Principles
      a. Ridge Line
      b. Sidewall
      c. Corners
   4. Pegs
      a. Types
      b. Set-up
      c. Alternatives
   5. Anchor Points
      a. Natural
      b. Artificial (i.e. poles)

6. Tarp Set-up Style
    a. A-frame
    b. Lean-to
    c. Flat top

C. Lesson Strategies

1. Using an **Interactive Lecture**, introduce the two different types of fabrics used to make tarps. Ask if people know the difference between both types of tarps (i.e., nylon & silicone coated nylon). Make them feel the difference in weight and to the touch. Explain the advantages of the silicone coated nylon tarp: (1) It is truly waterproof, (2) resistant to tearing, and (3) ultra-light. Then explain the disadvantages: (1) It is extremely flammable and (2) expensive (more than twice the price of a nylon tarp).

    Now present the advantages of the nylon tarp: (1) it is tear resistant and (2) inexpensive. The disadvantages: (1) It is heavier and (2) will absorb water. Also explain that both materials will still need to have any stitching sealed, but the silicone coated material needs a silicone-based sealant. Finally, explain that a group tarp should measure about 10' by 13' to accommodate 3 to 4 campers or two cooking groups if used as a cooking shelter.

2. Using a **Demonstration** teaching strategy, demonstrate how to set up an A-frame shelter using a tarp. Use a tree for one anchor point for the ridge line and a ski pole for the other end. Take the time to identify the parts of the tarp (1) ridge line, (2) sidewall, and (3) corners. Emphasize that the ridge line should be very tight and set high enough to allow campers to kneel underneath without touching the ridgeline. Indicate that the ridgeline rope will be

anchored to the tree using a bowline knot or a trucker's hitch.

Next demonstrate how to set up the other end of the ridge line using a ski pole. Indicate that it is helpful to use a clove hitch to anchor the ridge line rope to the ski pole and that the ski pole should be as close as possible to the tarp to avoid sagging on the ridge line.

When using a tent peg, indicate your peg selection for securing this stressful anchor point (i.e., using the largest peg available to increase surface of contact and strength). Make sure that you explain and demonstrate the correct position and angle for the peg (i.e., in line with the ridge line and at 45° with the head of the peg pointing away from the shelter) as well as some possible alternatives to the pegs such as roots, rocks or trees. Then create tension on the ridge line by using a trucker's hitch. Take the time to explain that the trucker's hitch is ideal for tarp set-up because it provides good tension can be readjusted quickly if the nylon stretches at night or when it is wet.

With the ridge line set up, ask volunteers to hold the four corners of the tarp and direct them on how to form an A-frame (four corners down), a Lean-to (two corners on the same side down and two corners on the other side up), and a Flat top (all four corners up). Ask students if they can explain the purpose of each type of shelter. Make sure that they associate the type of shelter with the right purpose. (1) A-frame: sleeping, (2) Lean-to: cooking with a view, and (3) Flat top: shading from sun.

Once the types of tarp have been demonstrated, continue your construction by setting up an A-frame shelter. Demonstrate how to secure the corners by explaining and demonstrating that a corner's rope must be pulled at 45° angle off the corner and anchored to an anchor via a trucker's hitch. Once you have completed all four corners show the various ways to secure the side ropes using natural anchors such as trees, rocks or roots.

3. Using a **Problem Solving Activity**, invite teams of 3 to 4 students to build an effective shelter. Assign a different shelter style to each team. Tell them that they only have 10 minutes to build their shelter before inspection. Once all of the shelters are built, have student groups review each one of them by looking and commenting on their shape, height, anchors, and knots. Praise their efforts and work when appropriate and ask each team to improve their set-up if appropriate.

D. Closure:
In closure, ask a few questions to assess student understanding.
- Ask if they can explain the purpose of each type of shelter.
- Ask what angle the corner ropes should be to avoid wrinkles in the sidewall.
- Ask what advantages silicone coated tarps have over nylon tarps.
- Ask why the trucker's hitch is used to anchor the tarp cords.
- Ask if anyone has any question or suggestions about how to effectively set-up a tarp?

III. Evaluation

A. Evidence of Student Learning:
Observing the students as they build various tarps should give you an opportunity to assess skills.

> Listening to students give each other feedback on different tarp set-ups will be helpful with formative assessment.
>
> Student answers to the closing questions will give you more information about their knowledge of tarp set-up.
>
> If you have time, perform a tarp Olympics to determine if the students can effectively set-up a tarp as an A-frame, lean-to or flat top.

Sample Lesson Plan for Teaching Content Knowledge

Instructor(s): Julie & Christian

I. Planning & Preparation

A. **Lesson Plan Title:** FLASH! - All About Lightning

B. **Educational Goals:** To help students understand the science of lightning and how to stay safe during a thunderstorm.

C. **Educational Objectives:** Students will be able to...
   1. Accurately explain how lightning works.
   2. Accurately explain where lightning strikes tend to occur.
   3. Accurately discuss ways to avoid danger from lightning.
   4. Accurately demonstrate what to do if a thunderstorm is approaching.
   5. Accurately demonstrate what to do if a thunderstorm is upon a group while hiking in different situations.
   6. Accurately demonstrate what to do if a thunderstorm is upon a group inside of tents.

D. **Student Preparation:**
   Student Background Knowledge:
   1. Students should have already learned the difference between a summit, exposed ridge, gulley, and forested area.
   2. It is helpful if students already know about weather patterns in the area that you are traveling through (mountain weather afternoon buildup, etc.).
   3. Students should know the difference between a subjective and objective hazard.

   Student Materials Needed:
   Ground pads

E.	**Instructor Materials Needed:** • 1 ski pole • Roll of athletic tape • Large rain coat • Plastic bag • Ground Pad • Backpack • Mylar sheet or white garbage bag • Dry erase markers (2) • 40 - 60 foot rope (2)
F.	**Duration:** 40 minutes
G.	**Location:** Open forest area
H.	**Foul Weather Alternative:** In case of rain, make sure that everyone has appropriate rain gear. If too extreme, teach fast and be directive (skip the "why" and go straight to **what to do for safety**). Relocate the group to a safe location.

II. Lesson Content and Methods

A.	**Creative Opening "Hook":** Have a student or instructor dressed as "Lightning" jump out in front of the group dressed in a cape (rain coat tied around neck) and a ski pole that shoots imaginary lightning. Introduce the topic and then have this super-charged character stay in the background until needed later in the lesson.

B.	**Body of Instruction:**
	Lesson Outline
	
	1. How lightning forms
	    a. Electrons & protons attracted
	    b. Overcome insulation
	    c. Lightning displaces air causing thunder
	2. Lightning is Dangerous
	    a. Ground Current

            b. Side Flash
            c. Upward Leaders
            d. Contact
            e. Direct Strike
            f. Blunt Trauma
        3. Lightning Safety (Preventative measures)
            a. Be familiar with mountain weather patterns (alpine start when necessary)
            b. Watch the weather and avoid high risk areas during signs of thunderstorms
            c. Be flexible & use good judgment
        4. High risk areas to avoid during thunderstorms
            a. Mountain tops
            b. High ridges
            c. Tall trees (higher than the others)
            d. Flat open terrain
            e. Shallow caves / overhangs
            f. Open water
            g. Tall trees at the edge of open water
        5. Safer places to go in the backcountry during a thunderstorm.
            a. Down! Down! Down!
            b. Lower ridge amidst trees of even heights
            c. Flat terrain amidst trees of even heights
            d. Depression in the landscape
        6. Safety details during a thunderstorm
            a. Avoid touching metal
            b. Insulate self from the ground
            c. Try to protect from elements

C. Lesson Strategies
    1. HOW LIGHTING FORMS: Using a **Demonstration** strategy that involves students, ask half of your students to step into the bottom of a mountain that

you "draw" on the ground using a rope. If you don't have a rope, draw it in the dirt or snow or create the mountain shape using natural materials. Give all of these students two small pieces of athletic tape to make the + symbol and then they can tape it to their front. These students represent positive charges (protons). Next, ask the other half of your students to step into a "cloud" that you "draw" above the mountain on the ground. Give all of these students a piece of athletic tape to attach to their front that represents the - symbol. These students are negative charges (electrons).

Next, explain that lightning occurs when electrons concentrate in the bottom of the cloud and become attracted to the protons in the ground. Ask students to move accordingly. The electron students should now all be at the bottom of the cloud and the proton students should be near the top of the mountain.

Continue narrating and ask students to move accordingly. "The atmosphere is a natural insulator. For lightning to form, the electric charge has to be big enough to overcome these insulating properties. When overcome, electrons flow down towards a high point (mountain top, tree, etc.) where protons have accumulated due to the pull of the thunderhead. When a connection is made, protons rush up to meet the electrons. This is the point that you see lightning and hear thunder." *Make a crashing noise by popping a bag full of air (that you have prepared in advance and hidden behind your back) as "Lightning" dramatically enters the scene and touches the mountain with the pole.*

Ask your students to hold up a thumb. Explain that a lightning bolt is only about 1" in diameter (or the size of a big thumb), but it is extremely long, so it displaces a huge amount of air.

Question students: What do you think happens when a huge amount of air is displaced at the speed of light?
Answer: Thunder!

2. LIGHTNING IS DANGEROUS. Use an **Interactive Lecture with Seeded Facts** teaching strategy to introduce the topic of how lightning can hurt us. Before your lesson you should have secretly handed six different students a fact card with a number on it. When you ask what the most common way lightning can hurt us, the person with Card #1 can share the information written. After the information is shared, elaborate or clarify any questions. Continue this pattern until all six fact cards have been shared. Use the information below to make the fact cards.

Seeded Fact Cards for Interactive Lecture with Seeded Facts

Card #1: Ground Current

Did you know that lighting can travel through the ground! Ground current is by far the biggest lightning hazard. It leads to 40%- 50% of all lightning fatalities. Keeping your feet close together can actually help minimize ground current exposure.

Card #2: Side Flash

Did you know that side flash is the next biggest lightning hazard contributing to 20%-30% of all lightning fatalities? Side flash occurs when lightning hits a tall object (such as a tree) and sends some of the current off to the side in an arc that looks for the path of least resistance to the ground (which can be people or animals). Avoiding tall trees or other objects will help keep you safer.

Card #3: Contact (Touch) Voltage

People and animals can also get hurt by touching a fence or post that gets hit by lightning. Contact voltage is less intense than a direct strike, but still contributes to 15% - 25% of lightning fatalities. To avoid contact voltage strikes, do not touch metal objects or objects that are not grounded during a thunderstorm.

Card #4: Upward Streamer (Leaders)

Well, did you all know that lightning can actually pulse up from an object in an upward streamer current? You don't even need to be close to the ground strike to be a conductor. These currents actually consist of 10% - 15% of lightning fatalities. In addition to avoiding high places, get as close to the ground as possible and crouch into a small ball to avoid launching a streamer current.

Card #5: Direct Strike

Direct strikes can send 20,000 amps of current through a body. Only about 3% - 5% of lightning fatalities are a result of direct strikes, so they are not very common. Avoiding high places and open areas during a thunderstorm are the best ways to avoid direct strikes in the backcountry.

Card #6: Blunt Trauma

Some people get injured when lightning hits an object and sends debris flying towards them. Avoid standing near large trees or other tall objects that have the potential to be conductors.

3. LIGHTNING SAFETY. For this part of the lesson, use a **Role Play** teaching strategy. To introduce ways to reduce risk of lightning injuries in the backcountry, meet before class with the students who you did not give seeded fact cards to. You can set the scenarios up so that there are two students on each scene. One follows the lightning safety strategies that you give and the other does not. For example, one student goes quickly down the mountain to safety when clouds move in, while the other lingers on top. The "Lightning" person swoops into the scene with a flash.

Set student up with scenarios of the following high-risk areas to avoid and safer places to go during thunderstorms:

    a. Mountain tops
    b. High ridges
    c. Tall trees (higher than the others)
    d. Flat open terrain
    e. Shallow caves / overhangs
    f. Open water
    g. Tall trees at the edge of open water

 4. LIGHTNING SAFETY PREVENTATIVE MEASURES. Use an **Interactive Lecture and Demonstration** with a more serious tone to review key points and emphasize safety. Emphasize that students should:
    a. Be familiar with mountain weather patterns (Alpine start when necessary)
    b. Watch the weather and avoid high risk areas during signs of thunderstorms
    c. Be flexible & use good judgment
    d. **Show** students how to crouch low on a ground pad with their feet together. Emphasize again that getting into a safer location is the best thing to do, but this position may be helpful to protect from ground currents.
    e. **Ask** how to calculate approximately how far away the heart of the lightning storm is from your current location. Answer: After the flash, count 5 seconds for every mile. Know that lightning can jump long distances.

D. **Closure:**

In closure, ask students a key question to assess understanding.
- What is the number one thing that you can do to minimize your risk of getting electrocuted during a thunderstorm in the mountains? (First, watch the weather and plan ahead. Next, find the safest nearby location if a storm moves in - off peaks and ridges, avoiding flat open areas of land and water, avoiding shallow caves, etc.).
- If you are in civilization, make sure to go inside a building or a car.

III. Evaluation

A. **Evidence of Student Learning:**
   Play a quick scenario game to assess an understanding of key safety concepts.
   - What do you do if you are near the top of a mountain and you see a thundercloud moving in? (Go down fast)
   - Should you ever take shelter under the tallest tree in the area? (No)
   - When a storm is intensely upon you and you are in a sheltered area in your tent, what can you do to minimize ground current exposure? (Sit on your ground pad with feet together).

Sample Lesson Plan for Teaching Values

| Instructor(s): Julie & Christian | |

I. Planning & Preparation

A. **Lesson Plan Title:** Why Care! Developing a Personal Land Ethic.

B. **Educational Goals:** To help students develop a personal land ethic.

C. **Educational Objectives:** Students will be able to...
   1. Demonstrate critical thinking.
   2. Be able to express personal values (able to articulate a personal land ethic).
   3. Identify specific ways to transfer Leave No Trace Principles to the front country.

D. **Student Preparation:**
   Student Background Knowledge:
   1. Students should have a thorough understanding of Leave No Trace (LNT) Principles.
   2. Students should have experience implementing Leave No Trace (LNT) Principles in the backcountry.

   Student Materials Needed:
   1. Journal & Pen

E. **Instructor Materials Needed:**
   - **Case Study** to read aloud
   - **Debate** procedures and format

F. **Duration:**
   50 - 60 minutes

G. **Location:**
   Comfortable Outdoor Location

H. **Foul Weather Alternative:**
   Set up a classroom tarp beforehand if the weather looks threatening and make sure that everyone has appropriate rain gear.

II. Lesson Content and Methods

A. Creative Opening "Hook":

Scenario idea: Walk into the outdoor classroom area in character using the **Theatrics** teaching strategy with your co-instructor. Pretend that you are walking down a street in the front country and dropping litter on the ground. Next, pretend to get into a huge truck and discuss your terrible gas mileage. Pretend to arrive at a gas station and get a Styrofoam cup and then fill snacks into as many plastic bags that you can. Discuss voting for a candidate who wants to destroy the EPA and eliminate national parks. Exaggerate!

B. Body of Instruction:

Lesson Outline

1. Share Ethical **Case Study**
2. Review Leave No Trace (LNT) Principles (1-minute quick skits)
    a. Plan Ahead and Prepare
    b. Travel and Camp on Durable Surfaces
    c. Dispose of Waste Properly
    d. Leave What You Find
    e. Minimize Campfire Impacts
    f. Respect wildlife
    g. Be Considerate of Other Visitors
3. *Debate* - Will following Leave No Trace Principles be enough to save the planet?
    a. Yes, follow them and apply parallel principles to the front country.
    b. No, we need to do much, much more and be proactive in addressing climate change.
4. Group *Discussion*
    a. What are things we can all do after arriving home to help the planet and its inhabitants?
5. Personal Reflection (journal)

a. Solo journaling

C. Lesson Strategies:

1. ETHICAL CASE STUDY: Using a **Case Study** teaching strategy, introduce a controversial land management issue in the area you are traveling through.

2. QUICK LEAVE NO TRACE (LNT) REVIEW. Using a quick **Skit** teaching strategy, break the students into partners or small groups and give them 1 minute to plan an LNT skit based on the principle that you assign them and 1 minute to present their skit to the group. This should not take more than 10 minutes. Move it along quickly and follow each principle up with a quick summary.

3. DEBATE. Use a **Debate** teaching strategy to trigger student analytical and critical thinking skills. The main *debate* question could be, **"Will following Leave No Trace Principles be enough to save the planet?"** Break the class into two groups (this could be based on views or done randomly), and then set up the procedures and explain the format before beginning. Remember, you are the moderator.

Break the class into two groups:
    a. **"Yes,"** follow the LNT principles and apply parallel principles to the front country.
    b. **"No,"** we need to do much more than just follow LNT principles and be proactive in addressing climate change.

Debate Procedures:
    Tone: Everyone should be cordial, use active listening and be respectful. Remind students that this is a class exercise and not a tavern screaming match.

Participation: Everyone on the team MUST participate.
Support: Groups should try to have 4 - 5 points to support their argument.

Debate Format: (Adjust for age level, group & goals)
- Opening Statement (1 minute each group)
- Present Positions (3 minutes each group)
- Rebuttal (5 minutes each)
- Closing Statement (1 minute each group)
- Open Comments

4. GROUP DISCUSSION. Use a **Group Discussion** teaching strategy to pull together the main points of the *debate* and reflect as a group on hopes and challenges. Use this strategy to help students think about transference and specific things they can all do to help the planet and its inhabitants after arriving home.

5. PERSONAL REFLECTION - JOURNALING. Use the **Personal Journaling** teaching strategy to give students some quiet space to reflect on their own after a potentially heated *debate*. This could be 5 minutes or longer as needed.

D. Closure:
In closure, ask students to regroup and share any personal insights that they have taken away from this lesson and the time they have spent in the backcountry.

III. Evaluation

A. Evidence of Student Learning:
The *debate* and group *discussion* should reveal student engagement, insight and growth. The closing activity when students share final thoughts could be especially helpful in assessing critical thinking and value clarification.

Outdoor Teaching Strategy Field Summary

Printed from *Outdoor Education Teaching Strategies* by Bisson & Bisson (2020)

Skill Oriented Teaching Strategies

1. **EDP-ECP (Level 8):** Explain – Demonstrate – Practice – Evaluate – Correct – Practice. An elaborate version of the classic 3 D's (Describe – Demonstrate – Do) often used to teach technical skills. *Application: Effective for teaching a simple knot such as a bowline.*

2. **Step by Step (Level 8):** Similar to the EDP-ECP, however it differs by breaking down the skill into small steps that all students perform at the same time with your guidance. *Application: Effective when teaching a complex knot such as the bowline on a coil.*

3. **Whole – Part – Whole (Level 8):** For complex skills. First you demonstrate the complete skill, then break it down into smaller parts using the EDP-ECP strategy, and finally put it all together to perform the whole skill. *Application: Effective when teaching an Eskimo roll.*

4. **Physical Manipulation (Level 8):** Best with a complex skill. Manually manipulate the movement of the student to help the learner acquire kinesthetic information about their body position. *Application: Effective when teaching a J-stroke on land or in the water.*

5. **Prompting Cues (Level 8):** Prior to the practice phase, associate a set of principles regarding the physical performance of a skill with a single cue word. Use the cue as needed while the student practices. *Application: Effective when teaching body position when climbing.*

6. **Video Feedback (Level 2):** Record student performance using a video camera and then show the video for immediate objective feedback about a performance. *Application: Effective when teaching cross-country skiing techniques such as a double pole push.*

Knowledge Oriented Teaching Strategies

7. **Interactive Lecture (Level 4):** Requires a prepared sequence of information no longer than 10 - 15 minutes during which time you ask questions that engage the audience. *Application: Effective when teaching a lesson on cloud families.*

8. **Lecture with Seeded Questions (Level 4):** Variation on interactive lecture. You give numbered questions to a few students before class with directions to ask each question at a specific time during the lecture. *Application: Effective when teaching a lesson on lightning.*

9. **Lecture with Seeded Facts (Level 4):** Variation on the lecture with seeded questions. Instead of questions, write facts on index cards and select a few students to share the fact at the appropriate time during the lecture. *Application: Effective when teaching about trees.*

10. **Lecture with Seeded Q-Cards (Level 4):** Write key words on index cards (Q-cards) and distribute them to all students. Students listen and fill in the blanks with their "key word" when appropriate. *Application: Effective when teaching a lesson on heat injuries.*

11. **Leapfrogging (Level 8):** Use when traveling through a changing landscape. Along the route prompt close observation by students as they analyze differences in environments. *Application: Effective when teaching plant adaptation.*

12. **Mystery Challenge (Level 4):** Students solve a problem through a series of questions that can only be answered with "YES" or "NO." They ask about possible reasons to explain the mystery. *Application: Effective when teaching about frost cracks on trees.*

13. **Demonstration (Level 3):** Support a mini-lecture by presenting a model, movement or prop to represent a concept in the lesson. *Application: Effective when teaching about extreme hazardous weather.*

14. **Skill Modeling (Level 7):** Works when students practice mimicking a skill in a contrived setting. *Application: Effective when using a mannequin to teach CPR.*

15. **Scale Modeling (Level 7):** Use when teaching difficult concepts such as geological time. Students experience abstract concepts on a human scale. *Application: Effective when teaching about the size of the solar system.*

16. **Guided Discovery (Level 4):** You have specific answers in mind for students to arrive at. You guide them to discover these answers through appropriate questioning. *Application: Effective when teaching LNT catholes using the "D's" of dumping (distance, depth, etc.)*

Value Oriented Teaching Strategies

17. **Quotes and Readings (Level 1):** Read a quote or a short text to inspire students or encourage reflection. *Application: Effective when teaching about Sigurd Olson.*

18. **Personal Journaling (Level 8):** Encourages reflection and exploration of ideas of interest to students. Often not shared but can also be used to establish a written dialog between you and the student. *Application: Effective when teaching about one's personal land ethic.*

19. **Group Journaling (Level 5):** Similar to the personal journaling but students write in one journal that is shared among the group. Students can reflect, take class notes or draw. *Application: Effective when sharing notes and quotes during a wilderness expedition.*

20. **Visual (Guided) Imagery (Level 1):** Ask the students to close their eyes and listen to a narration. Often, the narrative places the student at the center of the imagery. *Application: Effective when teaching about wilderness ethics.*

21. **Case Study (Level 5):** Use a summary of real-life events that occurred in the past while challenging students to provide solutions to avoid, correct, or respond appropriately to the event. *Application: Effective when teaching about decision making.*

22. **Nature Awareness Activities (Level 8):** Introduce different sensory activities that help students explore nature through touching, smelling, hearing, seeing or tasting. *Application: Effective when teaching about tree bark.*

Multi Oriented Teaching Strategies

23. **Art (Level 8):** Incorporate art into your lesson to help students conceptualize, problem-solve, problem-solve or practice a skill. *Application: Effective when teaching about animal adaptation and having students build a highly adapted creature out of natural materials.*

24. **Music (Level 8):** Hook students, embellish a lesson, reinforce content or demonstrate ways to boost morale by inviting students to create songs, sing songs, move to rhythms or dance. *Application: Effective when used to reinforce natural history content via student rap music.*

25. **Storytelling (Level 1):** Read or narrate a story aloud to your group. The stories can represent any genre. *Application: Effective when teaching about constellations and the Greek myths associated with them.*

26. **Student Storytelling (Level 5):** Invite students to create and share a mythical or fantasy story to explain a natural characteristic. *Application: Effective when teaching about the characteristics of a tree such as the Easter Hemlock small cones and drooping head.*

27. **Theatrics (Level 3):** You become a real life or fictional character. Dress up and use props as you interact with your students through dialogue and discussions. *Application: Effective when teaching about the life of a Voyageur.*

28. **Puppetry (Level 3):** Use puppets to teach lessons with you acting as a ventriloquist, interpreter or Sesame backstage puppeteer. *Application: Effective when teaching about natural history topics such as beaver behavior.*

29. **Student Puppetry (Level 6):** Empower your students to learn while becoming puppeteers. After researching a topic, reinforce learning by having small teams present "shows" to the rest of the group. *Application: Effective when teaching about endangered species.*

30. **Role-Play (Level 6):** Give a small group of students a specific scenario that they will act out for the rest of the students. The scrip should be written or carefully explained by the instructor. *Application: Effective when teaching a specific LNT principle.*

31. **Skits (Level 6):** Give a concept, idea or situation to a small group of students and ask them to improvise a short play that will be presented to the rest of the group. *Application: Effective when teaching about good and bad expedition behavior.*

32. **Role Modeling (Level 2):** Live and role-model the skills or values that you present to the students. This strategy is often used to reinforce desired behaviors. *Application: Effective when teaching how to dress for different conditions.*

33. **Discussion (Level 5):** Often framed as an open-ended question. You can use various techniques to encourage students to participate in this safe space. *Application: Effective when teaching about challenges leaders face when they emerge within a group.*

34. **Debate (Level 5):** Organize your students in small groups so that they can present an argument for or against an issue. Moderate the debate and agree upon rules. *Application: Effective when teaching about the impact of technology on a wilderness expedition.*

35. **Exploratory Learning (Level 8):** Students learn through exploration. They are guided by you when needed, but learning comes primarily through the student's own exploration. *Application: Effective when teaching about tree identification with a tree dichotomy chart.*

36. **Socratic Method (Level 4):** In this strategy, rather than "telling," you lead students to discover new concepts or values through a series of ordered questions. *Application: Effective when teaching about land stewardship.*

37. **Games (Level 5):** Any activity that involves competition, cooperation or social interaction through play that encourages students to apply, new knowledge or skills. *Application: Effective when teaching about different canoe strokes in a canoe tag game.*

38. **Problem Solving Activities (Level 5):** After teaching some basic principles, set up a real life or fictive problem and ask the students to solve it either individually or in a group. *Application: Effective when teaching about stove repair.*

39. **Simulation (Level 7):** This strategy places the students in a real-life situation and asks them to behave as if the events were real. Simulations happen in real time. *Application: Effective when teaching first aid skills.*

40. **Solo Experience (Level 8):** This strategy places the students in isolation in nature. A solo can last from a few minutes to a few days. *Application: Effective when teaching about self-reliance.*

41. **Peer Teaching (Level 8):** You teach a specific skill, knowledge or value to a small group of student and then ask them to teach the same lesson to other small groups of students. *Application: Effective when teaching camping related knots.*

42. **Service Learning (Level 8):** Involve your students in real life service experiences in which they will have to apply various new skills, knowledge or values. *Application: Effective when teaching about compassion.*

References

Bisson, C. & Luckner, J. (1996). Fun in learning: The pedagogical role of fun in adventure education. The Journal of Experiential Education, 19, 2, 108-112.

Bloom, B. (1956). *Taxonomy of educational objectives: The classification of educational goals.* (1st ed.). New York: Longmans, Green.

Brown, H. (1954). *The challenge of man's future: An inquiry concerning the condition of man during the years that lie ahead.* New York: Viking Press.

Caine, R., & Caine, G. (1991). Making connections: Teaching and the human brain. Alexandria, Va.: Association for Supervision and Curriculum Development.

Caine, R. N., & Caine, G. (1994). *Making connections: Teaching and the human brain.* Menlo Park, CA: Addison-Wesley Publishing Company.

Caine, R., & Caine, G. (1997). Unleashing the power of perceptual change: The potential of brain-based teaching. Alexandria, Va.: Association for Supervision and Curriculum Development.

Caine, R., & Caine, G. (2011). Natural learning for a connected world: Education, technology, and the human brain. New York: Teachers College.

Coleman, J.S. (1976). Differences between experiential learning and classroom learning. In M. T. Keeton (Ed.), *Experiential learning: Rationale, characteristics and assessment.* San Francisco, CA: Jossey-Bass.

Cornell, J. (1998). *Sharing nature with children: The classic parents' & teachers' nature awareness guidebook* (20th anniversary ed., 2nd ed., rev. and expanded ed., Sharing nature series, v. 1). Nevada City, Calif.: DAWN Publications.

Dweck, C. (2006). Mindset : The new psychology of success (1st ed.). New York: Random House.

Dale, E. (1969). *Audiovisual methods in teaching* (3d ed.). New York: Dryden Press.

Gagné, R., & Briggs, L. (1974*). Principles of instructional design.* New York: Holt, Rinehart and Winston.

Gardner, H. (1993). Multiple intelligences : The theory in practice. New York, NY: Basic Books.

Gardner, H. (1993). *Frames of mind: The theory of multiple intelligences* (10th anniversary ed.). New York, NY: Basic Books.

Gilbertson, K. (2006). *Outdoor education: Methods and strategies*. Champaign, IL: Human Kinetics.

Glasser, W. (1986). *Control theory in the classroom.* New York, NY: Harper & Row, Publishers.

Gookin, John (2016). Backcountry lightning risk management. Lander, WY. National Outdoor Leadership School.

Gullion, L. (1987). *Canoeing and kayaking: Instruction manual*. Springfield, VA: American Canoe Association.

Knapp, C. (1993). *Lasting lessons: A teacher's guide to reflecting on experience.* Charleston, WV: ERIC Clearinghouse on Rural Education and Small Schools.

Kolb, D. (1984). *Experiential learning: Experience as the source of learning and development* (First ed.). Englewood Cliffs, New Jersey: Prentice-Hall.

Maslow, A., & Frager, R. (1987*). Motivation and personality* (Third edition / ed.). New York: Harper and Row.

Pangrazi, R. (2007). *Dynamic Physical Education for Elementary School Children* (5th ed.). San Francisco: Benjamin Cummings.

Petzoldt, P., & Ringholz, R. (1984). *The new wilderness handbook* (Rev. and updated ed.). New York: Norton.

Priest, S., & Gass, M. (2005). *Effective leadership in adventure programming* (2nd ed.). Champaign, IL: Human Kinetics.

Priest, S., & Gass, M. (2018). *Effective leadership in adventure programming* (3rd ed.). Champaign, IL: Human Kinetics.

Redmond, K., Foran, A., & Dwyer, S. (2010). *Quality lesson plans for outdoor education*. Champaign, IL: Human Kinetics.

Smithhammer, B., & National Outdoor Leadership School (U.S.). (2005). *NOLS sea kayak instructor notebook*. Lander, WY: National Outdoor Leadership School.

Subramony, D., Molenda, M., Betrus, A., & Thalheimer, W. (2014). The mythical retention chart and the corruption of dale's cone of experience. Educational Technology, 54(6), 6-16.

Wagstaff, M., & Attarian, A. (2009). *Technical skills for adventure programming: A curriculum guide*. Champaign, IL: Human Kinetics.

Walter P. (2018). Learning theories: A new and complete approach to learning theories. Independently published.

About the Authors

Christian Bisson, (Ed. D.) is a professor of Adventure Education at Plymouth State University. He has taught skill and theory courses in higher education for nearly 25 years and has instructed in the outdoors for over 35 years. He has been a NOLS instructor since 1990, specializing in wilderness backpacking expeditions for outdoor educators.

Julie Gabert Bisson (M.A.) is a certified K-8 teacher who integrates creative outdoor teaching strategies daily into her fourth-grade curriculum at New Hampton Community School. She taught in higher education for 17 years and has been working as an outdoor expedition field instructor for over 30 years for various schools including NOLS.

Julie and Christian have hiked, paddled, climbed and caved all over the US, Canada, Australia, New Zealand, and Nepal. They live in New Hampshire where they go on adventures with their kids & dogs.

About the Illustrator

Meg McAndrew studies Adventure Education at Plymouth State University and is happiest when she is outdoors or doodling. Meg works at a non-profit promoting youth development through adventure where she combines her love for art and the outdoors by encouraging children to express their creativity through natural art.

Printed in Great Britain
by Amazon